COMPREHENSIVE RESEARCH
AND STUDY GUIDE

William B. Yeats

EDITED AND WITH AN INTRODUCTION
BY HAROLD BLOOM

BLOOM'S MAJOR SHORT STORY WRITERS

Anton Chekhov

Joseph Conrad

Stephen Crane

William Faulkner

F. Scott Fitzgerald

Nathaniel Hawthorne

Ernest Hemingway

O. Henry

Shirley Jackson

Henry James

James Joyce

D. H. Lawrence

Jack London

Herman Melville

Flannery O'Connor

Edgar Allan Poe

Katherine Anne Porter

J. D. Salinger

John Steinbeck

Mark Twain

John Updike

Eudora Welty

BLOOM'S MAJOR WORLD POETS

Maya Angelou

Robert Browning

Geoffrey Chaucer

Samuel T. Coleridge

Dante

Emily Dickinson

John Donne

T. S. Eliot

Robert Frost

Homer

Langston Hughes

John Keats

John Milton

Sylvia Plath

Edgar Allan Poe

Poets of World War I

Shakespeare's Poems & Sonnets

Percy Shelley

Alfred, Lord Tennyson

Walt Whitman

William Wordsworth

William Butler Yeats

William B. Yeats

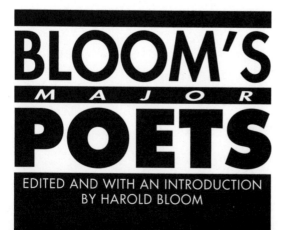

BLOOM'S *MAJOR* POETS

EDITED AND WITH AN INTRODUCTION
BY HAROLD BLOOM

© 2001 by Chelsea House Publishers, a subsidiary of
Haights Cross Communications.

Introduction © 2001 by Harold Bloom.

Printed and bound in the United States of America.

First Printing
1 3 5 7 9 8 6 4 2

Library of Congress Cataloging-in-Publication Data
applied for:

ISBN 0-7910-5936-7

Chelsea House Publishers
1974 Sproul Road, Suite 400
Broomall, PA 19008-0914

The Chelsea House World Wide Web address is
http://www.chelseahouse.com

Contributing Editor: Mirjana Kalezic

Produced by: Robert Gerson Publisher's Services, Santa Barbara, CA

Contents

User's Guide

This volume is designed to present biographical, critical, and bibliographical information on the author's best-known or most important poems. Following Harold Bloom's editor's note and introduction is a detailed biography of the author, discussing major life events and important literary accomplishments. A thematic and structural analysis of each poem follows, tracing significant themes, patterns, and motifs in the work.

A selection of critical extracts, derived from previously published material from leading critics, analyzes aspects of each poem. The extracts consist of statements from the author, if available, early reviews of the work, and later evaluations up to the present. A bibliography of the author's writings (including a complete list of all books written, cowritten, edited, and translated), a list of additional books and articles on the author and the work, and an index of themes and ideas in the author's writings conclude the volume.

~

Harold Bloom is Sterling Professor of the Humanities at Yale University and Henry W. and Albert A. Berg Professor of English at the New York University Graduate School. He is the author of over 20 books, including *Shelley's Mythmaking* (1959), *The Visionary Company* (1961), *Blake's Apocalypse* (1963), *Yeats* (1970), *A Map of Misreading* (1975), *Kabbalah and Criticism* (1975), *Agon: Toward a Theory of Revisionism* (1982), *The American Religion* (1992), *The Western Canon* (1994), and *Omens of Millennium: The Gnosis of Angels, Dreams, and Resurrection* (1996). *The Anxiety of Influence* (1973) sets forth Professor Bloom's provocative theory of the literary relationships between the great writers and their predecessors. His most recent books include *Shakespeare: The Invention of the Human,* a 1998 National Book Award finalist, and *How to Read and Why,* which was published in 2000.

Professor Bloom earned his Ph.D. from Yale University in 1955 and has served on the Yale faculty since then. He is a 1985 MacArthur Foundation Award recipient, served as the Charles Eliot Norton Professor of Poetry at Harvard University in 1987–88, and has received honorary degrees from the universities of Rome and Bologna. In 1999, Professor Bloom received the prestigious American Academy of Arts and Letters Gold Medal for Criticism.

Currently, Harold Bloom is the editor of numerous Chelsea House volumes of literary criticism, including the series BLOOM'S NOTES, BLOOM'S MAJOR DRAMATISTS, BLOOM'S MAJOR NOVELISTS, MAJOR LITERARY CHARACTERS, MODERN CRITICAL VIEWS, MODERN CRITICAL INTERPRETATIONS, and WOMEN WRITERS OF ENGLISH AND THEIR WORKS.

Editor's Note

My Introduction centers upon "The Second Coming," and argues that the poem's title is altogether misleading.

As there are 29 critical extracts in this volume, I confine myself here to noting only those I myself have found most useful.

Helen Regueiro on "The Wild Swans at Coole" presents remarkable insight.

On "Leda and the Swan," Thomas R. Whitaker elucidates Yeats's vision of history, with its cyclic patterns and extraordinary psychic overdeterminations.

"Sailing to Byzantium" receives commentaries by the distinguished critics Cleanth Brooks, Thomas R. Whitaker, and Richard Ellmann, while "Byzantium" is discussed by Whitaker and Ellman.

Yeats's death-poem, "Cuchulain Comforted," is read by this editor in the context of the Romantic tradition that helped mold Yeats.

Introduction

HAROLD BLOOM

From an early 21st century perspective, William Butler Yeats (1865–1939) appears to be the major Anglo-Irish poet in the long tradition that goes from Thomas Moore to our contemporary Seamus Heaney and beyond. No English poet of the last century, not even Thomas Hardy, D. H. Lawrence, or Geoffrey Hill, can be judged equal to Yeats in eminence. A handful of modern American poets— Robert Frost, Wallace Stevens, T. S. Eliot, Hart Crane—are of Yeats's stature, but cannot be said to surpass him. Time's revenges have been unkind to many of Yeats's social and political ideals, and to his occult enthusiasms, but his powers as a dramatic lyricist remain undiminished. Yeats recognized that Robert Browning was always a dangerous influence upon him, partly because both Yeats and Browning had swerved away from Shelley as prime precursor.

Robert Browning is now unfashionable, but is too great a poet not to return, once we get beyond the institutional politics of our bad moment, which prefers Browning's wife to him, and also exalts Mrs. Felicia Hemans as John Keats's equal, and Lady Mary Chudleigh as a rival to John Milton. But no one as yet prefers Charlotte Mew or Lady Dorothy Wellesley to W. B. Yeats, who thus seems in little danger of being demoted, except perhaps by the lunatic fringe of feminist critics, who after all do not flinch at castigating Shakespeare and Dante. Yeats's stance towards women is certainly archaic, being a curious blend of chivalry and brutality. But no one need take such attitudes seriously, since they are akin to Yeats's Fascist eugenics and his credulous table-rappings.

Yeats, as a poet, craved either ecstasy or wisdom, but luckily achieved something very different: a personal myth that plied him with powerful metaphors for his poetry. A convinced supernaturalist yet not a Christian, Yeats invoked spirits as so many variant muses, to enable his access to realms of vision where Shelley and William Blake had preceded him. He enters visionary space with less confidence than his Romantic precursors, and oddly enough also with less irony. The skeptical Shelley and the polemical Blake employ Biblical ironies to sound out their prophecies, but Yeats had little enough concern for the Bible, preferring the sacred scriptures of the East. Again, this benefited Yeats, for he was no prophet but a phantasmagorist. The intensity of Yeats's greatest lyrics is extraordinary, and is sustained by an intricate personal mythology, systematized in the two versions of *A Vision* (1925, 1937), in which the dead and history are reconciled as a cosmological dance of contraries.

Because of *A Vision*, Yeats is likely to seem a more difficult poet than he actually is. "The Second Coming," a chant of astonishing force, perplexes many readers because they assume the poem's title refers to Christ, which it does not. What is reborn and so comes again in Yeats's litany is the one-eyed male Egyptian Sphinx, God of the Sun. The poet hails him cognitively (though with a certain emotional revulsion) because this rough beast heralds the end of Christian revelation, and its replacement by the counter-revolutionary tide of Fascism. I don't know that a visionary Fascism is any more acceptable humanly than the terrifying brutalities of an actual Fascism, but "The Second Coming" is unquestionably a sublime poem, a triumph of language and of controlled turbulence.

Yeats makes legitimate demands upon his readers: we need always to pay close attention to his own relationship to what he sees and shows. As a dramatist of the self, Yeats towers above every other poet in the English language in the 20th century. We go back to his poetry incessantly, because we need that drama, and because its cognitive and passionate music overcomes all resistances. ❀

Biography of
William Butler Yeats

Though it is generally accepted that W. B. Yeats confided almost everything about his life and his experience in his manuscripts, diaries, and introductions to his works, the more we read about him, the more elusive he becomes. We cannot wholly trust his voluminous autobiographical writings, later collected in his *Autobiography*, because Yeats constantly constructed myths about himself. Although he spent much of his time trying to understand the contradictions in his mind, he rarely laid them bare. Yeats's obsessions with complex, esoteric philosophies that included magic, occultism, and mysticism, coupled with his strong Irish nationalism, make it difficult to construct a portrait of the poet.

William Butler Yeats was born in Sandynont, Dublin, on June 13, 1865. On his father's side his ancestry can be traced back well into the 18th century, showing a line of land-owning prosperity. His mother came from a prosperous merchant family, the Pollexfens, in Sligo, Ireland. When Yeats was two years old, his father, John Butler Yeats, abandoned the distinguished profession of barrister and moved his family to London so he could study painting. He also gave up his family's Christian faith (both his great-grandfather and his grandfather were parsons). John had been under the influence of the rationalism of John Stuart Mill and Auguste Comte, but after he went to London he spoke more often of William Blake and Walt Whitman, and he introduced his son to their poetry.

Because of financial difficulties, the Yeats moved back to Dublin in 1880, where W. B. Yeats attended high school. In 1883, he went to the Metropolitan School of Art in Dublin. He spent his holidays in Sligo, the setting of many of his poems.

Yeats's first publication, two short lyrics, appeared in the *Dublin University Review* in 1885. In the same year, he devoted himself to forming an occult group, the Dublin Hermetic Society. Yeats joined another group, the Theosophical Society, when he and his family went back to London in 1887, a year after he quit his art studies to pursue a writing career. Yeats didn't like the Age of Science and was far more interested in the mysticism of astrology than the concreteness of astronomy; it seems quite natural that the

Theosophical Society, a growing international movement that sought wisdom through mysticism, fascinated him.

The year 1889 was a watershed for Yeats. His early poems, collected in *The Wanderings of Oisin and Other Poems*, were published and very favorably received. Oscar Wilde was one of the reviewers who praised the volume. In addition, Yeats made the acquaintance of poet William Morris, whose influence he acknowledged throughout his career. Also, that same year Yeats met Maud Gonne, with whom he fell deeply in love. Unfortunately, his sentiments were not returned; that was when, as he himself remarked later, "the troubling of [my] life began." Yeats soon became involved in the Irish nationalist cause, partly because it was Maud Gonne's chief passion. The young poet felt that Irish political life could achieve more significance if filled with art, poetry, drama, and legend.

By the 1890s, Yeats was already something of a celebrity in the London literary and artistic scene. In 1891, he founded "The Rhymers Club," one of the most well-known groups of fin-de-siècle poets; among its members were poets whom Yeats later called "the tragic generation": Lionel Johnson, Ernest Dowson, John Davidson, and Arthur Symmons. He made several trips to Paris, becoming familiar with modern French poetry; on one trip, he met the French poet Paul Verlaine, whom he admired. Throughout Paris, the belief in "art for art's sake" (*l'art pour l'art*) was at its height. An additional important influence of this period was Yeats's intensive study of Blake's poems, which he undertook in collaboration with Edwin Ellis. This led to an edition of Blake's poetry in 1893. *The Wind among the Reeds*, Yeats's next volume of poetry, came out in 1899.

In 1896 Yeats met an ally in the Irish nationalist cause, Augusta Lady Gregory, an aristocrat who collected old stories, the lore of west Ireland. Her friendship sustained him until her death in 1932. From 1897 on, Yeats spent his summers at Coole Park, Lady Gregory's home. Yeats believed that literature could help engender a national unity that would be capable of transfiguring the Irish nation. With Lady Gregory's help, Yeats established an Irish national theater. This ultimately led to the founding of the famous Abbey Theater in Dublin. Yeats wrote the play *On Baile's Strand* for the theater's opening night in 1904, and he devoted himself to the daily tasks of running the Abbey for several years afterward.

Between 1902 and 1908, presumably because of his involvement with theater life, Yeats wrote only a few lyrics. He also began a process of "remaking" himself, a modification rather than a new orientation, that would possess him for the next 37 years. (In his seventies he wrote a marvelous lyric on this theme, "Myself must I remake.")

He traveled to Italy with Lady Gregory in 1907, visiting Florence, Milan, Urbino, and Ravenna. His yearning for Renaissance Italy reverberated throughout his work of this period. In 1913, Yeats engaged Ezra Pound as his secretary, and the two poets would significantly influence each other. The following year, Yeats published another volume of poems, *Responsibilities*, which contains poems written over a long period of time, 1907–1914.

Gradually, Yeats noticed that the Abbey Theater seemed to be losing its soul, since many of the plays struck Yeats as being vulgar. Soon he would encounter a new kind of drama. In the winter of 1915, Pound was translating Japanese Nô plays. Yeats found them to be a perfect blend of words, masks, dance, and music. He wrote several plays, including *At the Hawk's Well* (1916), in the style of Nô drama.

After being rejected several times by Maud Gonne, who eventually married a "man of action" (an Irish soldier, Major John MacBride), Yeats wedded Miss Georgie Hyde-Lees in 1917. *The Wild Swans at Coole*, another volume of poetry, was published that year. The couple's daughter, Ann Butler Yeats, was born in 1919, and a son, William Michael Yeats, in 1921.

In the 1920s, Yeats achieved political as well as literary success. In 1922, when the Irish Free State was established, he became a senator. Already a very esteemed international literary figure, he was awarded the Nobel Prize for Literature in 1923 (which he did not decline, as he had an offer of knighthood in 1915). Two years later, Yeats presented his meditation upon the relationship between imagination and the occult in the prose work *A Vision*, which was first published in 1925 and revised into its final form in 1937. Much of the symbolism of Yeats's later poetry would rely on the historical and philosophical system that the poet explicated in *A Vision*.

The Tower (1928), one of Yeats's strongest collections of poems, named after a ruined Norman castle he bought at Gort, was enthusiastically received by the critics and sold very well. As early as

1900, writing of Shelley's use of the tower symbol, Yeats saw the tower as a symbol of "a mind looking inward upon himself."

Yeats continued writing through his sixties with a persistent intensity of feelings. With his leanings towards authoritarian ideology, it has often been charged that he was a Fascist during his last years. (It is true that he admired Italian Fascist dictator Benito Mussolini for his vigor.) *The Winding Stair and Other Poems* appeared in 1933. In the five years that followed, after the often-ill poet underwent a Steinach rejuvenation operation in 1934, Yeats produced four verse plays; the poetry collection *A Full Moon in March* (1935); an edition of the *Oxford Book of Modern English Verse 1892–1935* (1936); and the final revision of *A Vision*. His *Last Poems* were published posthumously, after he died in southern France in 1939. Final arrangements for his burial in Ireland couldn't be made until 1948, after World War II, when his body was finally taken to Sligo.

Yeats devoted much of his work to the exploration of the sometimes heartbreaking contradictions between life and death, creating a brave acceptance of the whole spectrum of human experience. His own epitaph, addressing those subjects, was engraved on his tomb:

Cast a cold eye
On life, on death.
Horseman, pass by! ❀

Thematic Analysis of
"The Wild Swans at Coole"

Most of the poems in the volume *The Wild Swans at Coole* were written between 1915 and 1917. The title poem was written in 1916 and first published in 1917, two or three months after Maud Gonne again refused Yeats's marriage proposal. Yeats was then a 51-year-old bachelor who had pursued Maud Gonne with "almost ridiculous continuity" for 27 years.

"The Wild Swans at Coole" is written in a mood of intense feeling, of depression; however, the depression is of a different kind than what is expected in light of Gonne's persistent refusal. What grieves the poet is not that he is refused once again, but that he is not crushed by his loss of passion.

The poem belongs to the tradition of what M. H. Abrams has called the "Greater Romantic Lyric," in which a speaker in a landscape undergoes "an out-in-out process in which mind confronts nature and their interplay constitutes the poem." Typical of this tradition, the poem resonates with the influence of Wordsworth's *Tintern Abbey*, as in the line "trod with a lighter tread," which unmistakably recalls "like a roe / I bounded o'er the mountains." The poem's other link to the Romantic tradition is with Shelley's *Alastor*, in which the lover's unhappiness is intensified by envisioning the joy of mated swans.

"The Wild Swans at Coole" is written in the first person, and the opening stanza gives a splendidly composed vision of an actual landscape in autumn: the trees, the woodland paths, the water at Lady Gregory's Coole Park. The poet sets the scene before introducing his persona in the second stanza. He announces, with scientific precision, that exactly 59 swans are now on the lake. Then the poet reveals that he has tried to count the swans for 19 autumns. The first time he tried, he now remembers, they scattered away before he finished his count.

In the third stanza, the changes the poet has undergone between the ages of 32 and 51 are measured with the sudden realization that his longing for a particular woman has faded. The poet creates an emotional contrast between the present, when his "heart is sore" and his initial drive and enthusiasm have spent themselves, and the past, when he trod with a lighter tread.

As many critics have remarked, the swans may be seen as a symbol for ideal lovers, since swans mate for life. "All's changed" is contrasted with the swans' constancy of feeling, their immutability, as described in the fourth stanza: "unwearied still, lover by lover." Their "hearts have not grown old," the poet adds. Two of Yeats's other poems, written in the same period, spring from the same seed. In "Living Beauty" (1915) the poet exclaims,

> O Heart we are old
> The living beauty is for younger men:
> We cannot pay its tribute of wild tears,

and in "A Song" he chants,

> O who could have foretold
> That the heart grows old?

The original order of the stanzas in "The Wild Swans at Coole" was 1-2-5-3-4, so that the first version of the poem ended with the fourth stanza and the ambiguous word "still," which can mean both "motionless" or "continuing." The word "still" resonates throughout the poem: "a still sky," "unwearied still," "attend upon them still," and "the still water." Critic Richard Ellmann observes in his book *The Identity of Yeats* that "by putting the third stanza at the end Yeats emphasized his personal deprivation in time, and made possible the symbolic reading that his awakening would be his death, a paradox well within his boundaries."

By rearranging the stanzas, Yeats changed the emphasis of the poem, perhaps to make it more bearable for himself. Some critics feel that the change weakened the poem. Comparison of the two versions leads to some interesting questions: What is the difference in effect between the two versions? Does the poem benefit from the change? Which one is aesthetically better? Every reader must determine the answer for him or herself. ❀

Critical Views on
"The Wild Swans at Coole"

DONALD STAUFFER ON "THE WILD SWANS AT COOLE"

[Donald Stauffer (1902–1952) is the author of *Art of Biography in Eighteenth Century England* (1941), *Nature of Poetry* (1946), and *Poetry and the Easy Life* (1948). In this extract taken from his book on Yeats, he discusses different approaches to the poem.]

Since the achievement of poetry marks the worth of poetic theory, let us turn to a single lyric poem and read it in the light of Yeats's thought. Consider "The Wild Swans of Coole" (1919). ⟨. . .⟩

Like all the luckiest poems, this can be read with enjoyment on any of many levels. Often it gets into the anthologies, where readers may legitimately consider it as a pleasing poem on a pretty subject. The technical analysts and metrists may savor the contrasts between its feminine and masculine line-endings, may speculate on the uses of its two pairs of half rhymes, and above all may be delighted by the unanalyzable rhythm of its lines.

Those who believe a poem is self-sustaining and explicable only in its own words and form will also find rewards in "The Wild Swans"—in Yeats's cunning and almost invariable linking of each stanza to its predecessor by some repeated word or thought which modifies into a new development. They will note that the poem begins with the swans upon the lake, shifts to the images of the swans in the air, and returns to the swans on the lake—a perfect round. They will find structure in the antitheses between the swans and their beholder, and between the beholder now and the beholder nineteen years ago. And they will note (let us hope) that the essential pattern is not built in time but in a contrast between moods, and that since only mortal man in this poem feels such contrasts, the founding antithesis is between transient man and eternity.

Those who like comparative judgments may occupy themselves profitably in the parallels between the building of this poem and of, for instance, Keats's "Ode to a Nightingale." In structural devices for meditative poems of about this length, Keats and Yeats are as similar as their names.

—Donald Stauffer, *The Golden Nightingale* (New York: The Macmillan Company, 1949): pp. 64–66.

⊕

EDWARD ENGELBERG ON THE METAPHORICAL IMPLICATIONS OF THE POEM

[Edward Engelberg is a professor of comparative literature at Brandeis University. He is the author of numerous articles and, in addition to *The Vast Design,* from which this extract is taken, of *The Symbolist Poem: The Development of the English Tradition* (1967); *The Unknown Distance: From Consciousness to Conscience, Goethe to Camus* (1972); and *Elegiac Fictions: The Motif of the Unlived Life* (1989). Here he discusses the inadequacy of literal speculations about the poem.]

In these earlier volumes, up to *The Wild Swans at Coole* (1919), a little past the midpoint in his career, Yeats has obviously been groping. Time and memory, past and present, dream and reality, occur with frequency, and often traditionally, but already there are signs of a developing mode, namely the poetic voice which recognizes the strength of presence by focussing on absence. It is not, however, until the title poem, "The Wild Swans at Coole," that Yeats writes a major sustained organic poem which develops all the motifs he had previously brushed in lightly. This poem and others in this volume—"In Memory of Major Robert Gregory," "The Fisherman," "Broken Dreams," "Presences," "Upon a Dying Lady," "Ego Dominus Tuus"—develop conceits on the motif of presence and absence, each slightly different, each a preparation for some of the grand monumental poems that followed in subsequent volumes.

In "The Wild Swans at Coole" Yeats (the poet) observes the swans long enough to count them (fifty-nine) and to recall how many years he has come to see them (nineteen)—in short, long enough to make us realize the event is telescoped, not a sudden one time episode. Hence everything is in a sense to be read as doubled, the event and its metaphorical implications. Literal speculations about the poem have run into problems. Yeats says that before he had "well finished" his count he saw the swans "All suddenly mount" and scatter. If that were so how could he render such a specific count? The answer is that the counting is a function of time past (and passed) and time present; that the fifty-nine swans are in a sense the sum total of repetition over many years, and their sudden flight into "great broken rings" signifies not an interruption but a phase beyond the past, a reminder of the present which flows into history at the very moment it also forges into the future. For Yeats understands that the presence of the swans and their precipitous flight have stopped his ability to recount their number—is it fifty-nine, or more, or less, *this* time? For this time he cannot finish his count; or to put it more metaphorically, the present has suddenly interfered with the normal sense of counting, that is, with time. Not only the swans but the years he has observed them are given a number. The interruption brings him to a phrase repetitious almost verbatim from "Easter 1916"—"All's changed. . . ." Now youth—absence—is retrieved; the swans are back in the water paddling with young hearts, not this year's swans but the swans of all time. The thought of the past invoked by the present now unfolds a future, and in almost a reversal of Keats's musings about the emptied town, Yeats imagines the presence of swans emptied of himself as observer:

> Among what rushes will they build,
> By what lake's edge or pool
> Delight men's eyes when I awake some day
> To find they have flown away?

The speculation is not of another life after his (the poet's) death so much as the power of time itself, the irresistible curiosity of contemplating both the presence of the poet and the (temporary) absence of the swans, as they fly away, and the eventual presence of the swans and the absence of the poet. Yeats is on the way towards a genuinely holistic perception.

—Edward Engelberg, *The Vast Design* (Washington, D.C.: The Catholic University of America Press, 1964): pp. 228–29.

CURTIS B. BRADFORD ON THE "A" DRAFT OF THE POEM

[Curtis B. Bradford is the author or editor of several books on Yeats, among them *Yeats at Work* (1965) and *W. B. Yeats: The Writing of the Player Queen* (1977). In this extract from *Yeats at Work,* he analyzes the "A" draft of the poem.]

In the years following the publication of *The Wind Among the Reeds* Yeats wrote very few lyric poems. During the decade 1899–1909 most of his energy went into the Irish dramatic movement. With others he founded the Irish Literary Theatre in 1899, became president of the Irish National Theatre Society in 1902, and after December 27, 1904 was at times almost immersed in the affairs of the Abbey Theatre. His own writing centered in an exploration of subjects derived from Irish heroic legend in a series of plays and narrative poems. Plays exploiting Irish legend included *Cathleen ni Houlihan* (1902), *On Baile's Strand* (1903), *The King's Threshold* (1904), and *Deirdre* (1907); narrative poems such as "The Old Age of Queen Maeve" and "Baile and Aillinn" make a somewhat different use of similar materials. Yeats also wrote much prose during these years; the expanded *Celtic Twilight* appeared in 1902, *Ideas of Good and Evil* in 1903, the rewritten *Stories of Red Hanrahan* in 1904, *Discoveries* in 1907. In December 1908 Yeats began the Journal from which he later extracted "Estrangement" and "The Death of Synge."

These activities caused Yeats early in 1909 to wonder seriously if he would continue to grow as a poet. It was on February 25 that he wrote the journal entry which he slightly revised in "Estrangement XXXVIII":

> I often wonder if my talent will ever recover from the heterogeneous labour of these last few years. The younger Hallam says that vice does not destroy genius but that the heterogeneous does. I cry out vainly for liberty and have ever less and less inner life. . . . I thought myself loving neither vice nor virtue; but virtue has come upon me and given me a nation . . . Has it left me any lyrical faculty? Whatever happens I must go on that there may be a man behind the lines already written; I cast the die long ago and must be true to the cast.

At about the same time Yeats wrote in "All Things can Tempt me"

> All things can tempt me from this craft of verse;
> One time it was a woman's face, or worse—

The seeming needs of my fool-driven land;
Now nothing but comes readier to hand
Than this accustomed toil.

Yeats's talent did recover from the heterogeneous. He emerged from these activities a capable manager of theater business, a successful propagandist, and a better poet. Why Yeats's engulfment in the heterogeneous had this last effect we shall perhaps never certainly know. The ways of genius are not entirely explicable, but it is clear that bad luck had made his life interesting which meant that Yeats had more to say, and it is also clear that a decade spent in writing largely for the theater had given him wide experience in developing and handling a seemingly colloquial style. Whatever the causes, shortly after writing the laments quoted above Yeats in 1909 began once more frequently to write lyric poems, now nearly always personal utterances. The man behind the lines was a changed man with a changed conception of the nature and purpose of art. During the years 1909–19 he was to write many of his greatest poems. ⟨. . .⟩

The manuscripts of poems included in Yeats's next collection, *The Wild Swans at Coole* (1917), are likewise for the most part late drafts, and again there are not in Mrs. Yeats's collection any manuscripts at all of some of the finest poems, such as "In Memory of Major Robert Gregory" and "The Double Vision of Michael Robartes." This is all the more to be regretted since beginning in 1915 and 1916, in poems such as "Ego Dominus Tuus," "The Wild Swans at Coole," and "Easter 1916," Yeats experienced a breakthrough to a greater art than he had hitherto created. Fortunately the manuscripts of "The Wild Swans at Coole" do show that poem in various stages of its creation.

Yeats's general mood, his cast of mind was reminiscent and nostalgic, though an Irish event like the revolution of 1916 could, as always, arouse his interest in an occasion. He had recently finished "Reveries over Childhood and Youth" and was continuing his autobiography in the manuscript known as "First Draft" which brings the story of his life up to 1898. It is natural that Yeats while meditating on his youth should begin his questioning of old age. This theme now moves into the very center of his poetry; in October 1916 Yeats finished "The Wild Swans at Coole," one of his greatest poems on old age. In this characteristic work Yeats uses what is nearest to him and most familiar, a walk along Coole Water, to express a universal state of mind and emotion. As he does this he achieves a diction and a rhetoric that can rightly be called noble.

Three successive drafts of the poem have survived. In all of them the order of the stanzas is as in the first printing of the poem with what is now the last stanza in the middle of the poem, following line 12. Draft A must have been written very early in the process of composition, since Yeats completed only four lines of his poem in this draft; draft B is transitional, that is it grows directly out of A and moves toward draft C; here Yeats completed thirteen lines and the whole of his original last stanza; by the end of draft C Yeats had nearly finished his poem. ⟨. . .⟩

Before he began work on draft A Yeats had established his stanza form, perhaps in still earlier drafts which have not survived. In this stanza three long lines—they range in the finished poem from eight to eleven syllables—alternate with three short lines of five, six, or seven syllables. The basic pattern seems to my ear to place four stresses against three with a variation of five against three at each fifth line and occasionally elsewhere. The stanza has the unusual rhyme scheme abcbdd. It has not occurred before in Yeats's poetry and does not exactly recur, though many years later Yeats used this rhyme scheme but not the pattern of line lengths in "Three Songs to the Same Tune" and the related "Three Marching Songs." The arrangement of the rhymes varies the ababcc pattern that was a favorite scheme with Yeats. The stanza pattern described above governs everything Yeats does in the drafts.

—Curtis B. Bradford, *Yeats at Work* (Carbondale: Southern Illinois University Press, 1965): pp. 43–44, 48–49.

⟨∿⟩

HAROLD BLOOM ON THE LINK BETWEEN SHELLEY AND YEATS

[In this excerpt from his book on Yeats, Harold Bloom, the editor of this series, discusses the influence of Shelley's *Alastor* and later poems on Yeats's "The Wild Swans at Coole."]

The title poem, dated October 1916, rises from the complex mood in which Yeats began what was to be his last solitary year of bachelorhood. As Jeffares indicates, the poem's dominant emotion is not frustrated longing for Maud Gonne, but sorrow that the poet's passion for her is dead. A man of fifty-one looks upon the same scene he saw at thirty-two. He comes to the scene again after having proposed marriage again to the same woman as nineteen years before, and after being refused, yet again. But his primary awareness is not of a dismal, almost ridiculous continuity, between an earlier and a later self. Discontinuity dominates, for the depression of nineteen years before was at the refusal, but the depression of 1916 is for *not* feeling depression at the continued refusal. His heart has grown old, and its soreness is that it should have aged.

This pattern is inherited indirectly from *Tintern Abbey.* Wordsworth both longs for and does not desire the raptures of an earlier phase, when he later returns to a crucially remembered landscape. Judiciously he balances loss and gain, the means of balance being the compensatory imagination, with its deeper autumnal music and sober coloring rising to take the place of a fled ecstasy. Between Wordsworth, who always evaded Yeats, and *The Wild Swans at Coole*, the essential link is the ambivalent Wordsworthianism of Shelley in *Alastor* and later poems, from the hymns of 1816 down to the death poem of 1822, *The Triumph of Life. Alastor*, as many critics have suggested, is a major source of *The Wild Swans at Coole*, which is perhaps the first poem in which Yeats swerves crucially away from the Shelleyan quest for the *daimonic* beloved. Of the two possibilities allowed by *Alastor*'s Preface, life burned away by the self-consuming quest or the heart burning coldly to the socket, Yeats fears now to have fulfilled the latter. When the doomed Poet, in *Alastor*, reaches the sea-shore, he begins to apprehend the desolation stalking him in the shape of his *alastor* or Spirit of Solitude. This apprehension follows the Poet's Spenserian vision of a solitary swan:

> A strong impulse urged
> His steps to the sea-shore. A swan was there,
> Beside a sluggish stream among the reeds.
> It rose as he approached, and with strong wings
> Scaling the upward sky, bent its bright course

High over the immeasurable main.
His eyes pursued its flight.—"Though hast a home,
Beautiful bird; thou voyagest to thine home,
Where thy sweet mate will twine her downy neck
With thine, and welcome thy return with eyes
Bright in the lustre of their own fond joy.
And what am I that I should linger here,
With voice far sweeter than thy dying notes,
Spirit more vast than thine, frame more attuned
To beauty, wasting these surpassing powers
In the deaf air, to the blind earth, and heaven
That echoes not my thoughts?"

This same passage from *Alastor* is a crucial influence upon *The Tower*, as will be shown later. In *The Wild Swans at Coole*, Yeats recalls it for deliberate contrast, for his depression and apparent loss is that he no longer shares this vision of the relation between poet and swan. The Poet of *Alastor* sees in the swan an emblem of the subjective quest, but the quest realized as he, the Poet, never can realize it, precisely because his greater powers cannot be fulfilled by the inadequate context of nature, with its deaf air, blind earth, and unechoing heaven. Yeats too sees in the swans his *antithetical* quest fulfilled, but his regret is that for him the passionate or outward-bound aspect of the quest is forever over. It is of considerable critical importance that the stanza acknowledging this, now the fourth of five in the poem, was in the poem's first appearance the final stanza, so that the plangency of accepted defeat ended the poem:

Unwearied still, lover by lover,
They paddle in the cold
Companionable streams or climb the air;
Their hearts have not grown old;
Passion or conquest, wander where they will,
Attend upon them still.

Evidently, Yeats chose at first to put his emphasis here, upon his ancient love for Maud, the central passion of his life, being extinct. In revision, he took the poem's central stanza, and placed it last, altering absolutely the poem's significance:

But now they drift on the still water,
Mysterious, beautiful;
Among what rushes will they build,

By what lake's edge or pool
Delight men's eyes when I awake some day
To find they have flown away?

Ellmann speculates that, by putting this stanza at the end, "Yeats made it possible to read it symbolically so that his awakening would be his death." This is possible, but unnecessarily stretched. Awakening here is not death but the end of *antithetical* consciousness, the complete breaking with the Shelleyan influence. The prophecy was not fulfilled, perhaps because such an awakening would have been a death-in-life for Yeats, even after love was dead.

—Harold Bloom, *Yeats* (New York: Oxford University Press, 1970): pp. 190–93.

⊗

HELEN REGUEIRO ON YEATS'S ATTEMPT TO COME TO TERMS WITH LOSS

[Helen Regueiro is the author of the book *The Limits of Imagination: Wordsworth, Yeats, and Stevens* (1976), from which this excerpt is taken. Here she discusses the discontinuity of the self in time in Yeats's poem and Wordsworth's *Tintern Abbey*.]

This keen perception of the finiteness of things gives "The Wild Swans at Coole" its poignant beauty. The poem is, in a sense, Yeats's "Tintern Abbey," though without the ultimate resolution and affirmation that Wordsworth brings to his poem:

The trees are in their autumn beauty,
The woodland paths are dry,
Under the October twilight the water
Mirrors a still sky;
Upon the brimming water among the stones
Are nine-and-fifty swans

The peacefulness and fulfillment in the natural scene of the first stanza underscore the tension felt by the poet within the temporal perspective. The stillness and fruition of autumn provide the occasion for the poet's wearied look at the lack of stillness and fruition in his life. Yet the anger against time which comes through in other poems is muted here into a quiet resignation. Returning to the same scene nineteen years after, Yeats finds that all is changed. The swans are "unwearied still," but the assertion of continuity within the natural perspective serves to underline, as in "Tintern Abbey," the discontinuity of the self in time. The description of the swans points to the opposite though unuttered description of the poet: "*Their* hearts have not grown old; / Passion or conquest . . . / Attend upon them still" (my italics). The stillness of the autumn landscape is repeated adverbially and projected into a temporal landscape, suggesting recurrence and continuity. The connection between the temporal and the natural in "Tintern Abbey" pointed to a pattern of quiet restoration. The stillness which unites both realms here serves to distinguish the temporal self from the natural perspective in which such unity exists. The still sky of the opening stanza is mirrored by the still water of the last. But the poet mirroring himself in time against a previous encounter discovers that for him there is no stillness, temporally or naturally, in the fullest meaning of the term. The swans, still there, unwearied still, seem untouched by, impervious to the temporal world. But the poet perceives their movements in "great broken rings." Recurrence and continuity—captured in the double meaning of "still"—refer to a world no longer there. The poet's encounter forces him to recognize, simultaneously, the pastness of the past and the impossibility of the present encounter in the future. There is no "life and food / For future years" here. In Stevens' "Description without Place" "swans far off [are] swans to come," the apocalyptic vision spanning past and future in a placeless and timeless perspective. But the future in Yeats's poem holds only the expectation of swans that have flown away:

> But now they drift on the still water,
> Mysterious, beautiful;
> Among what rushes will they build,
> By what lake's edge or pool
> Delight men's eyes when I awake some day
> To find they have flown away?

The last stanza does not destroy the stillness and the continued presence of the swans, but it does project the poet from the distance of his present encounter to a further distance in time. The magic stillness of the autumn landscape is not broken. But the poet, unable to be fully drawn into the natural enchantment, finds himself moving in "great broken rings." Like Wordsworth in "Tintern Abbey," Yeats begins by telling time in terms of seasons ("The nineteenth autumn has come upon me") but ends by seeing the seasons projected into an abstract, temporal world. There is no Dorothy in this poem to contain the temporalization of the natural. The faint presence of Maud Gonne in fact accentuates the estrangement of the poet's encounter. He "counts" the seasons as he counts the swans, and the counting is in a strange sense already the "awakening" of the last stanza, the inability to move within the wheeling rings of the swans.

Like "Tintern Abbey," "The Wild Swans at Coole" is an attempt to come to terms with loss. Occasionally, Yeats refuses to do so, and in the guise of a mad or at least an eccentric protagonist he rebels against the inevitability of change: "I spit into the face of Time / That has transfigured me." Memory here functions quite differently than in "The Wild Swans at Coole." It becomes a mode of transcendence, a refutation of the temporal perspective within which it exists. There is in this poem ("The Lamentation of the Old Pensioner") an acknowledgment of change and, simultaneously, a refusal to consider its finality. Memory, abstractive and transcendent, redeems the self from the negative transfiguration it is faced with.

—Helen Regueiro, *The Limits of Imagination: Wordsworth, Yeats, and Stevens* (Ithaca: Cornell University Press, 1976): pp. 100–102.

Thematic Analysis of
"The Second Coming"

This poem, written in January of 1919, is usually considered the central poem of the Yeats canon. As early drafts that Mrs. Yeats rescued from a wastebasket show, the poem initially alluded to the disquieting political events of 1916 through 1919. However, during the conception of the poem, Yeats deliberately eliminated all topical references to the Great War, the overthrow of the Russian czar in 1917, and the Russian Revolution, replacing them with the more expansive vision of his 2000-year-cycle theory of history. He was familiar with the Theosophists' belief that a new god comes at regular intervals to replace the old god, and he found this cyclical god theory particularly effective for his poetry.

Yeats mischievously took the shocking title from Christian doctrine and the Bible's prediction of Christ's second coming in Matthew 24, and the poem alludes to St. John's vision of the beast of the Apocalypse in Revelation. If we add to this the birthplace of Bethlehem cited at the end of the poem, the place almost always associated with Jesus' infancy, we can understand why so many critics are misled in finding solely Christian parallelisms in the poem. However, the poem actually illustrates Yeats's belief that the violent, apocalyptic events of his time heralded a change in god, and that the 2000-year reign of Christianity was about to end.

There is overwhelming power and sweeping force, even a sense of foreboding, in the opening image of the falcon and the falconer:

> Turning and turning in the widening gyre
> The falcon cannot hear the falconer.

Yeats's falcon, who in the first drafts of the poem was a hawk, travels in a gyre; this cone-shaped, spiral movement was an important symbol in Yeats's philosophical system. The lines echo Dante's description in *The Inferno* of how he and Virgil arrive at the eighth circle of Hell seated on the monster Geryon's back.

Critics do not agree on what the falcon may represent; A. N. Jeffares thinks that the falcon represents man, while Harold Bloom argues that the falconer, rather than the falcon, stands for man, "and the falcon represents his mastery of nature, now in the act of falling apart."

The next line pronounces the obvious: "Things fall apart; the centre cannot hold." The strength of this statement is achieved by a caesura in the middle of the line.

In lines 7 and 8 of the poem,

> The best lack all conviction, while the worst
> Are full of passionate intensity,

Yeats echoes Shelley's *Prometheus Unbound*:

> The good want power, but to weep barren tears,
> the powerful goodness want.

We are prepared in the first stanza for the ominous event of the second stanza, but we expect that the Second Coming will be Christ's reappearance. But instead, "a vast image out of *Spiritus Mundi*," Yeats's "general storehouse of images which have ceased to be a property of any personality or spirit," appears. A sphinx-like figure, with a lion's body and a man's head (more like the Egyptian sphinx at Giza than a Greek sphinx, which was female), "is moving its slow thighs," after 20 centuries of slumber.

> Surely some revelation is at hand;
> Surely the Second Coming is at hand.
> The Second Coming! Hardly are those words out
> When a vast image out of *Spiritus Mundi*
> Troubles my sight: somewhere in sands of the desert
> A shape with lion body and the head of a man,
> A gaze blank and pitiless as the sun,
> Is moving its slow thighs, while all about it
> Reel shadows of the indignant desert birds.
> The darkness drops again; but now I know
> That twenty centuries of stony sleep
> Were vexed to nightmare by a rocking cradle,
> And what rough beast, its hour come round at last,
> Slouches towards Bethlehem to be born?

The poet establishes the awesome, dark atmosphere of the poem through word choice and imagery. Primarily, the words "desert birds," with their forbidding aspect as birds of prey, "darkness," "stony sleep," "nightmare," "slouches," (which carries much of the poem's strength), and "rocking cradle" all demand our imagination's rapid response. Secondly, the image comes from *Spiritus Mundi*, a sort of human racial memory, indicating its universal origin. Furthermore, we witness the beast's nightmarish awakening and moving towards "the rocking cradle" of Christianity. This final intimation makes the poem exceptionally alarming and its apocalyptic tone justified.

"The Second Coming" has inspired a flood of critical comments, ranging from the harsh judgment that it prophesies the coming of fascism, to the opposite view that the poem is religiously prophetic rather than political. The close association between the poem's imagery and the main ideas of *A Vision* makes it difficult to interpret. However, Richard Ellmann and other critics have suggested that the poem has a prophetic authority of its own. By retaining a general diction ("anarchy," "innocence," "the best," "the worst"), Yeats elevates the poem to the visionary realm. ❁

Critical Views on
"The Second Coming"

[In this extract, W. B. Yeats discusses his theory of history.]

Robartes copied out and gave to Aherne several mathematical diagrams from the *Speculum,* squares and spheres, cones made up of revolving gyres intersecting each other at various angles, figures sometimes of great complexity. His explanation of these, obtained invariably from the followers of Kusta-ben-Luki, is founded upon a single fundamental thought. The mind, whether expressed in history or in the individual life, has a precise movement, which can be quickened or slackened but cannot be fundamentally altered, and this movement can be expressed by a mathematical form. A plant or an animal has an order of development peculiar to it, a bamboo will not develop evenly like a willow, nor a willow from joint to joint, and both have branches, that lessen and grow more light as they rise, and no characteristic of the soil can alter these things. A poor soil may indeed check or stop the movement and a rich prolong and quicken it. Mendel has shown that his sweet-peas bred long and short, white and pink varieties in certain mathematical proportions suggesting a mathematical law governing the transmission of parental characteristics. To the Judwalis, as interpreted by Michael Robartes, all living mind has likewise a fundamental mathematical movement, however adapted in plant, or animal, or man to particular circumstance; and when you have found this movement and calculated its relations, you can foretell the entire future of that mind. A supreme religious act of their faith is to fix the attention on the mathematical form of this movement until the whole past and future of humanity, or of an individual man, shall be present to the intellect as if it were accomplished in a single moment. The intensity of the Beatific Vision when it comes depends upon the intensity of this realisation. It is possible in this way, seeing that death is itself marked upon the mathematical figure, which passes beyond it, to follow the soul into the highest heaven and the deepest hell. This doctrine is, they contend, not fatalistic because the mathematical figure is an expression of the mind's desire, and the more rapid the development of the figure the greater the freedom of the soul. The figure while the soul is in the body, or suffering from the consequences of that life, is frequently drawn as a double cone, the narrow end of each cone being in the centre of the broad end of the other.

It had its origin from a straight line which represents, now time, now emotion, now subjective life, and a plane at right angles to this line which represents, now space, now intellect, now objective life; while it is marked out by two gyres which represent the conflict, as it were, of plane and line, by two movements, which circle about a centre because a movement outward on the plane is checked by and in turn checks a movement onward upon the line; & the circling is always narrowing or spreading, because one movement or other is always the stronger. In other words, the human soul is always moving outward into the objective world or inward into itself; & this movement is double because the human soul would not be conscious were it not suspended between contraries, the greater the contrast the more intense the consciousness. The man, in whom the movement inward is stronger than the movement outward, the man who sees all reflected within himself, the subjective man, reaches the narrow end of a gyre at death, for death is always, they contend, even when it seems the result of accident, preceded by an intensification of the subjective life; and has a moment of revelation immediately after death, a revelation which they describe as his being carried into the presence of all his dead kindred, a moment whose objectivity is exactly equal to the subjectivity of death. The objective man on the other hand, whose gyre moves outward, receives at this moment the revelation, not of himself seen from within, for that is impossible to objective man, but of himself as if he were somebody else. This figure is true also of history, for the end of an age, which always receives the revelation of the character of the next age, is represented by the coming of one gyre to its place of greatest expansion and of the other to that of its greatest contraction. At the present moment the life gyre is sweeping outward, unlike that before the birth of Christ which was narrowing, and has almost reached its greatest expansion. The revelation which approaches will however take its character from the contrary movement of the interior gyre. All our scientific, democratic, fact-accumulating, heterogeneous civilisation belongs to the outward gyre and prepares not the continuance of itself but the revelation as in a lightning flash, though in a flash that will not strike only in one place, and will for a time be constantly repeated, of the civilisation that must slowly take its place. This is too simple a statement, for much detail is possible. There are certain points of stress on outer and inner gyre, a division of each, now into ten, now into twenty-eight, stages or phases. However in the exposition of this detail so far as it affects the future, Robartes had little help from the Judwalis either because they cannot grasp events outside their experience, or because certain studies seem to them unlucky. "'For a time the power" they have said to me,' (writes Robartes) "'will be with us, who are as like one another as the grains of sand, but when the revelation comes it will not come to the poor but to the great and learned and establish again for two thousand years prince & vizier. Why should we resist? Have not our wise men marked it upon the sand, and it is because of these marks, made generation after generation by the old for the young, that we are named Judwalis.'"

Their name means makers of measures, or as we would say, of diagrams.

—W. B. Yeats, "Michael Robartes and the Dancer," in A. Norman Jeffares, *A Commentary on the Collected Poems of W. B. Yeats* (Stanford: Stanford University Press, 1968): pp. 239–41.

⊛

JON STALLWORTHY ON YEATS'S ALTERATION FROM "HAWK" TO "FALCON"

[Jon Stallworthy is the author of *The Astronomy of Love* (1961) and *British Poets of the First World War* (1988). This excerpt is taken from his book on Yeats, *Between the Lines*, published in 1963. Here he contrasts different drafts of the poem.]

Ellmann dates this poem January 1919, although it was not published until November 1920, in *The Dial*. Manuscripts in Mrs. Yeats's possession show how large a part the world situation of 1918–19 played in its conception and growth. There are six small, loose-leaf sheets of preliminary manuscript working, and two fair copies, the earlier of which Yeats tore in half and committed to his waste-paper basket: from this Mrs. Yeats recovered it.

'The Second Coming' begins with a tantalizingly illegible prose draft. Of its twelve lines I can read in the first five:

F. I r: *Ever more wide sweeping gyre*

Ever further hawk flies outwards

from the falconer's hand. surely

(   ) *fallen who*

when the mob (   )

In the remaining six lines one word only stands out, in splendid isolation at the opening of line nine: 'Burke.' Below this passage the iambic pentametres begin:

intellectual gyre is (   )
The ~~gyre grow wider and more~~ *wide*
falcon cannot hear
The ~~hawk can no more hear~~ *the falconer*

~~The germans to Russia to the place~~

The germans are (   ) now to Russia come

Though every day some innocent has died

(   ) *& murder*

⟵———⟶   ⟨...⟩

An important alteration is that from 'hawk' to 'falcon.' Ellmann is right when he says:

> The image of the falcon who is out of the falconer's control should not be localized, as some have suggested, as an image of man loose from Christ; Yeats would not have cluttered the poem by referring to Christ both as falconer and as rocking cradle further on.

The falcon has long been a problem. Once, however, we realize that the bird was originally a hawk, we are on familiar territory. As a boy Yeats had often 'climbed Ben Bulben's back,' which he describes in *The Celtic Twilight* as 'famous for hawks,' and his footnote to 'Meditations in Time of Civil War' is immediately relevant:

I suppose that I must have put hawks into the fourth stanza because I have a ring with a hawk and a butterfly upon it, to symbolize the straight road of logic, and so of mechanism, and the crooked road of intuition: 'For wisdom is a butterfly and not a gloomy bird of prey.'

It is 'The intellectual gyre' that is growing 'wider and more wide.' We are told in *A Vision*: 'As Christ was the *primary* (objective) revelation to an *antithetical* (subjective) age, He that is to come will be the *antithetical* revelation to a *primary* age.' And again: 'When our historical era approaches . . . the beginning of a new era, the *antithetical* East will beget upon the *primary* West and the child or era so born will be *antithetical*.' The 'gloomy bird of prey' has slipped its leashes, and will soon be lost to sight. In this first verse-draft Yeats follows a symbolic reference with a more topical and specific one: 'the germans are (   ) now to Russia come.' By the end of July 1917 the Russian front had crumbled in face of the enemy. In October of that year the Bolsheviks brought off their revolution, and at the Treaty of Brest-Litovsk, on 3 March 1918, Lenin had surrendered to the Germans: Finland, Esthonia, Courland, Lithuania, and tracts of Russian Poland. The Germans had indeed come to Russia, and I think it not impossible that Yeats, with his reverence for the aristocratic virtues epitomized by Castiglione, had in mind the fate of the Russian Royal House, as he wrote: 'Though every day some innocent has died.' ⟨. . .⟩

Considering now the completed poem as an artistic whole, we find that most common Yeatsian pattern of an objective first movement passing into a more subjective second movement. There is a natural division between lines 8 and 9, like that dividing the octave of a Petrarchan sonnet from the sestet. Incantatory repetition prepares us for the change:

Surely some revelation is at hand;
Surely the Second Coming is at hand.
The Second Coming!

The prophet comes into the open: 'a vast image. . . . Troubles my sight:.' Having described the image he sums up:

but now I know
That twenty centuries of stony sleep
Were vexed to nightmare by a rocking cradle,

Just as Yeats never wrote a love poem that does not treat of lover as well as of beloved, we are not allowed to overlook the figure of the prophet behind the prophecy.

Only two or three months elapsed between the writing of 'The Second Coming' and 'A Prayer for my Daughter,' and not for nothing did Yeats have them printed next to each other. Both, it will be seen, stem from a mood of depression brought on by the First World War, although, in both, references to the conflict are made less explicit in the manuscript drafts. The two poems have also a 'cradle' and a theme in common. 'The ceremony of innocence is drowned' is an idea explored at greater length in 'A Prayer for my Daughter':

> How but in custom and in ceremony
> Are innocence and beauty born?

—Jon Stallworthy, *Between the Lines: Yeats's Poetry in the Making* (Oxford: Oxford University Press, 1963): pp. 17–19, 24–25.

⊛

HELEN HENNESSY VENDLER ON "THE SECOND COMING" AS THE POEM OF MENTAL EXPERIENCE

[Helen Hennessy Vendler is the A. Kingley Porter University Professor at Harvard University. Her books include *On Extended Wings: Wallace Stevens's Longer Poems* (1969), *Part of Nature, Part of Us* (1981), *The Odes of John Keats* (1983), and *The Given and the Made: Strategies of Poetic Redefinition* (1996). In this extract taken from her book on Yeats, published in 1963, she gives us a psychological rather than a historical interpretation of the poem.]

It has not been generally recognized, I think, that Yeats, for all his fascinated horror, *approves* intellectually, if not emotionally, of the Second Coming. "When I was a boy," Yeats writes in *Wheels and Butterflies*, "everybody talked about progress, and rebellion against my elders took the form of aversion to that myth. I took satisfaction in certain public disasters, felt a sort of ecstasy at the contemplation of ruin . . . I began to imagine . . . a brazen winged beast that I associated with laughing, ecstatic destruction." The destruction of the known is always a terrifying experience; and the clutching of the familiar is the greatest deterrent to new knowledge. "The Second Coming" is a poem of intellectual acceptance and emotional retreat; the two attitudes produce the curious conflict in tone. The terror of the unique outdoes, finally, the horror of the original anarchy, simply because anarchy is known, historically and personally, and has been coped with before, while the Beast forebodes an entirely new experience. The Deluge is a familiar symbol, and so is disintegration:

> Things fall apart; the centre cannot hold;
> Mere anarchy is loosed upon the world,
> The blood-dimmed tide is loosed, and everywhere
> The ceremony of innocence is drowned.

The original Deluge, we recall, did not drown "the ceremony of innocence," but rather came to cleanse corruption, and this is the characteristic function of mythical cataclysms. Yeats's world, however, is not being destroyed out of wrath, but out of necessity. There is no agency at work, no God repaying with vengeance. The ceremony of innocence is drowned by a tide of anarchy which, though evil and murderous in itself, is nevertheless historically innocent, acting as an agent of inevitable historical necessity. Yeats makes this clear in "A Prayer for My Daughter," written close in time to "The Second Coming" and immediately following it in the *Collected Poems*. Yeats paces in his tower,

> Imagining in excited reverie
> That the future years had come,
> Dancing to a frenzied drum,
> Out of the murderous innocence of the sea.

Innocence is opposed to innocence: the purging innocence of blind matter in the sea yet destroys the evolved "innocence" of civilization, which is a very sophisticated thing, the delight of the soul in itself:

> . . . All hatred driven hence,
> The soul recovers radical innocence,
> And learns at last that it is self-delighting,
> Self-appeasing, self-affrighting,
> And that its own sweet will is Heaven's will . . .
>
> How but in custom and in ceremony
> Are innocence and beauty born?

It is a piece of consummate trickery on Yeats's part, in one sense, to give destroyer and destroyed the identical name of "Innocence." We should not forget that for him the word has overtones from Blake. In the *Songs of Innocence,* the word has several reaches of meaning, the first being the obvious one of a state unviolated by experience, but the others having to do with a state beyond experience (as, for example, in "The Little Girl Lost," "Night," "The Little Black Boy"). So, in Yeats, the Rough Beast represents one variety of innocence, a blind, primitive sort. He symbolizes, literally, a new birth, a passing to another level, leaving behind all that has been developed and refined in the old state. The Beast is a world-restorer, like the Spirit that moved upon the Waters, like Noah on Mount Ararat, and like the Messiah; but while the biblical and classical accounts of world renewal celebrated the beauty of the fresh world, Yeats has nothing to say of a Golden Age. The fertility of the Fourth Eclogue, the rainbow of Genesis, the gifts of the Magi, have no part in the Yeatsian comment on the renewal of experience; his *Parousia* takes place in a desert, whose attributes ("a gaze blank and pitiless as the sun") are transferred to the Beast. There is likewise no place for the ideal beauty which is often a corollary of renewal. Christ, traditionally, was ideally formed according to artistic canons of harmony, and Virgil's "parve puer," smiling at his mother, lies in a cradle full of flowers. Yeats's Beast, however, is a monstrous slouching combination of lion and man, enigmatic as the Sphinx, but without the monumental grandeur of statuary.

If, as we have said, the Great Year is Yeats's guarantee that poetic springs will not fail, then the Second Coming, being one of the manifestations of the several recurrences that make up the Magnus Annus, must be a symbol to us of the nature of Yeatsian inspiration. The Beast is no conventional Muse, certainly, and we may momentarily be as indignant as the desert birds at its sudden hulking appearance. However, the poem is in every sense the narrating of a vision which reveals new knowledge:

> A vast image out of *Spiritus Mundi*
> Troubles my sight . . .
> The darkness drops again; but now I know
> That twenty centuries of stony sleep
> Were vexed to nightmare by a rocking cradle.

For twenty centuries (during the primary Christian civilization) the antithetical Beast has slept like a granite sphinx; now somewhere the cradle has been set rocking for it and its sleep, turned to nightmare, has been broken. Translated out of the historical symbolism, the images would seem to mean that some event has triggered one variety of imagination from its dormant state into sudden and violent activity, as the poem begins its struggle to be born. If this seems a farfetched interpretation, we have only to look at Yeats's comment on coming revelation: "Why should we believe that religion can never bring round its antithesis? Is it true that our air is disturbed, as Mallarmé said, by 'the trembling of the veil of the Temple,' or 'that our whole age is seeking to bring forth a sacred book'?" To bring forth not a Savior, not a Restorer, in any personal sense, but "a sacred book." It does not matter that we can be amused at Yeats's credulity in thinking *Louis Lambert* and *Seraphita* the sacred books he had been waiting for. What is revealing is that for Yeats the Second Coming is on one level at least a literary phenomenon.

I have spent so much time on "The Second Coming" because it illustrates very well the poetic use to which Yeats put materials from *A Vision,* and moreover, it is a poem which has been given, in most commentaries, an exclusively historical or esoteric interpretation rather than a psychological one. It seems to me not so much a poem about Fascism, or about war, as about mental experience, and while the First World War may have provided symbols, it hardly provided the core.

—Helen Hennessy Vendler, *Yeats's* Vision *and the Later Plays* (Cambridge, Mass.: Harvard University Press, 1963): pp. 99–102.

℘

THOMAS R. WHITAKER ON THE MAGICAL SYSTEM OF PROPHECY IN THE POEM

[Thomas R. Whitaker is a professor at Yale University and author of a book on William Carlos Williams (1968), as well as *Mirrors or Our Playing: Paradigms and Presences in Modern Drama* (1999). In this extract taken from his study on Yeats, *Swan and Shadow: Yeats's Dialogue with History* (1964), he explains Yeats's magical system of prophecy.]

> Turning and turning in the widening gyre
> The falcon cannot hear the falconer . . .

The strangely compelling quality of those opening lines of "The Second Coming" arises partly from the fact that the orderly operation of centrifugal force (mimed in the assonance pattern) produces uncontrollable disorder. Because the falcon cannot resist the momentum of the gyre movement, it becomes a dangerous agent of violence—a central paradox of determinism and freedom in Yeats's vision of history.

> Things fall apart; the centre cannot hold;
> Mere anarchy is loosed upon the world,
> The blood-dimmed tide is loosed, and everywhere
> The ceremony of innocence is drowned;
> The best lack all conviction, while the worst
> Are full of passionate intensity.

The central problem posed by that forceful summary, according to R. P. Blackmur, is its apparently double source: in Yeats's "magical" system of prophecy and in his observation of the modern world. By what coincidence did both lead to the same conclusion? However, an understanding of Yeats's dialogue with history causes that problem largely to disappear, for the "magic" that I have been describing was not a separate field of investigation but a means of coping with a psychic reality which includes, as one aspect, the correlated schisms in state and soul. Yeats did not simply combine an external analysis of contemporary history with concepts drawn from his "instructors"—or (for that matter) from Pater's account of the gain of centrifugal over centripetal in Plato's day, or from the Delphic Oracle's description of "the bitter waves of blood-drenched life," or from his own description of the inundating sea in "Rosa Alchemica." He presented with new understanding the psychological and ethical opposites long implicit in his own subjective dialogues.

> The best lack all conviction, while the worst
> Are full of passionate intensity.

Though the language may derive from Shelley, the lines render and judge an evil known through conversation with an interior Lucifer.

This speaker, of course, focuses more clearly upon the social macrocosm than earlier speakers have done, because Yeats's alchemical path has spiraled toward greater inclusiveness. From that basis in mordant perception can now arise the vision itself—with its stammering beginning, its sweeping and somberly weighted climax, and its terrifyingly certain and yet uncertain conclusion:

> And what rough beast, its hour come round at last,
> Slouches towards Bethlehem to be born?

Though the beast has symbolic ancestors—Blake's Orc awakening after eighteen centuries of sleep, the Black Pig visiting blissful destruction upon an exhausted world, the uncontrollable mystery on the bestial floor—it paradoxically transcends them all. It is no herald of an ideal era but the compensatory image which *Spiritus Mundi* or the unconscious sends to one who, himself a mixture of the uncertain "best" and the passionate "worst," hopes for a Second Coming. It slouches as an incompletely specified "shape," its blank and pitiless gaze and its slow thighs conveying more, in juxtaposition to the cradle of Bethlehem, than do all Yeats's systematic explanations. But we are not left with flaccid resignation. The final lines are spoken by one who can maintain his questioning stance even when nearly overpowered by that image erupting from the abyss of himself and of his time.

—Thomas R. Whitaker, *Swan and Shadow: Yeats's Dialogue with History* (Chapel Hill: The University of North Carolina Press, 1964): pp. 73–74.

Donald Davie on the Calculated Collision in the Poem

[In this essay, Donald Davie (1946–1988) argues that the poem is clearer when read with the rest of the collection than when read alone.]

Each of these poems gains greatly from being read in the context of the others; and thus *Michael Robartes and the Dancer*, no less than other collections by Yeats, illustrates Hugh Kenner's contention that 'he was an architect, not a decorator; he didn't accumulate poems, he wrote books.'

How this works can be seen best with what may seem to be the most dubious case among those I have cited, 'Easter 1916.' This poem is clearer when read in the collection that it is when read in isolation, because only in the collection does one see why the woman involved in the 1916 Rising is given pride of place over the male leaders who paid for their participation with their lives. And, to take another example, those who read 'The Second Coming' in the *Nation* for 6 November 1920, or in *The Dial* for that same month, missed a dimension of the poem which appears when it immediately precedes 'A Prayer for My Daughter'; 'a rocking cradle' in the third line from the end takes on poignancy, and witnesses to personal involvement, when taken along with 'this cradle-hood and coverlid' in the second line of the poem which succeeds it—the ominous prophecy made in 'The Second Coming' is uttered, we are made to realise, by a man whose newborn child gives him a stake in the tormented future he prophetically sees. ⟨...⟩

In his Introduction to *The Resurrection* (*Wheels and Butterflies*, 1934), after Yeats has told how as a boy he 'took satisfaction in certain public disasters, felt a sort of ecstasy at the contemplation of ruin,' he asks himself:

> Had I begun *On Baile's Strand* or not when I began to imagine, as always at my left side just out of the range of the sight, a brazen winged beast that I associated with laughing, ecstatic destruction?
>
> *(Explorations)*

And he adds in a footnote: 'Afterwards described in my poem "The Second Coming."' But, of course, it is not described in 'The Second Coming,' where the beast is neither winged nor brazen:

> The Second Coming! Hardly are those words out
> When a vast image out of *Spiritus Mundi*
> Troubles my sight: somewhere in sands of the desert
> A shape with lion body and the head of a man,
> A gaze blank and pitiless as the sun,
> Is moving its slow thighs, while all about it
> Reel shadows of the indignant desert birds.

It may be that we are refusing to read the poem which Yeats intended to write; but we can do no less, for the intention was never fulfilled. And if we follow the introduction to *The Resurrection* any farther, we find ourselves blurring this memorable and masterly poem into unsatisfactory Nietzschean plays of Yeats's youth, where a brazen beast is also seen in vision.

The two 'technical' terms in the 'The Second Coming'—'gyre' and '*Spiritus Mundi*'—ought not to obscure the fact that the poem, as it stands in *Michael Robartes and the Dancer*, is self-explanatory. Poetically, all the meaning of the poem is in the calculated collision in the last line of the words 'slouches' and 'Bethlehem':

'Slouches towards Bethlehem to be born . . .'

What the poem says is that when the superhuman invades the human realm all that the human can say of it is that it is non-human: there can be no discriminating at such a time between subhuman and superhuman, between bestial and divine. Whatever further gloss the poem may need can best be supplied by the poem which immediately follows it, 'A Prayer for My Daughter,' which takes up from 'The Second Coming' not just 'cradle' but also 'ceremony,' also 'innocence.' From a human point of view a time-scale of solar years can never be so affecting as a scale of decades, and those readers were surely not wrong who found the poem piercingly relevant between 1939 and 1945.

—Donald Davie, "*Michael Robartes and the Dancer*," in *An Honoured Guest: New Essays on W. B. Yeats*, ed. Denis Donoghue and J. R. Mulryne (New York: St. Martin's Press, 1966): pp. 73–74, 78–79.

Thematic Analysis of
"Leda and the Swan"

Yeats wrote this brilliantly intense lyric in a disguised Italian sonnet form in 1923 and regarded it as one of his major accomplishments. Interestingly enough, Yeats printed "Leda and the Swan" as an introductory poem to the "Dove or Swan" section of *A Vision*, in which he discusses his cyclical theory of history. In a note following its publication in 1924, he explained that

> [I] wrote Leda and the Swan because the editor [George Russell] of a political review asked me for a poem. I thought 'After the individualist, demagogic movement, founded by Hobbes and popularised by the Encyclopaedists and the French Revolution, we have a soil so exhausted that it cannot grow that crop again for centuries.' Then I thought 'Nothing is now possible but some movement or birth from above, preceded by some violent annunciation.' My fancy began to play with Leda and the Swan for metaphor and I began this poem; but as I wrote, bird and lady took such possession of the scene that all politics went out of it, and my friend tells me that his conservative readers would misunderstand the poem.

In almost all versions of the Greek myth the poem is based on, Zeus is attracted to the mortal Leda and seduces her in the form of a swan. Some versions maintain that the offspring of this encounter were Pollux and his twin brother Castor; others, more rarely, claim it was Clytemnestra, the wife of Agamemnon. But most accounts assert that Helen of Troy, whose beauty led to the devastating Trojan war, is the child of this seduction. In *A Vision*, Yeats also mentions two eggs of Leda, from which came Love and War.

Zeus's action is usually described in polite euphemisms, such as "visited" and "seduced," but Yeats decided to give vigorous prominence to the physical technicalities of the act as a rape. This also may be evidence, as critic William H. O'Donnell has remarked, that "he had begun rehearsing his later role as the 'Wild Wicked Old Man' of a 1938 poem."

The explosive opening is achieved by breaking the first line in two halves: "A sudden blow: the great wings beating still." The line also attains a fine effect of diction with the pun on "still."

While previous drafts of the poem show a predominantly narrative structure, the final version is more graphic ("the staggering girl," "thighs caressed," "helpless breast," "loosening thighs"):

> Above the staggering girl, her thighs caressed
> By the dark webs, her nape caught in his bill,
> He holds her helpless breast upon his breast.

The second stanza asks two rhetorical questions:

> How can those terrified vague fingers push
> The feathered glory from her loosening thighs?
> And how can body, laid in that white rush,
> But feel the strange heart beating where it lies?

In the next stanza, the irrepressible stress on physicality in "A shudder in the loins engenders there" is followed by the gently flowing line "the broken wall, the burning roof and tower," and then a magnificent closing of the stanza with a full stop in midline: "And Agamemnon dead." It is Yeats's extraordinary conception that the "shudder in the loins" engenders the future. Zeus had begotten not only Helen, but the whole consequence of Helen's existence as well: the fall of Troy and the eventual deaths of the Greek heroes, one of them being Agamemnon.

A mysterious final question ceremoniously closes the poem, in which Yeats asks if the act of joining the divine and the human serves only the gods or if it also bestows divine insight on the human.

> So mastered by the brute blood of the air,
> Did she put on his knowledge with his power
> Before the indifferent beak could let her drop?

The poem is highly valued by most critics, and unquestionably its extraordinarily skillful orchestration of language and its rhetorical triumphs deserve praise. ❈

Critical Views on
"Leda and the Swan"

GIORGIO MELCHIORI ON THE GENESIS OF THE POEM

[Giorgio Melchiori is the author of *Joyce in Rome: The Genesis of Ulysses* (1984). His most recent work is *Italian Studies in Shakespeare and His Contemporaries* (1999). This extract is taken from his book *The Whole Mystery of Art.* Here he discusses the genesis and symbolism of the poem.]

A sudden blow: the great wings beating still
Above the staggering girl, her thighs caressed
By the dark webs, her nape caught in his bill,
He holds her helpless breast upon his breast.

How can those terrified vague fingers push
The feathered glory from her loosening thighs?
And how can body, laid in that white rush,
But feel the strange heart beating where it lies?

A shudder in the lions engenders there
The broken wall, the burning roof and tower
And Agamemnon dead.
                              Being so caught up,
So mastered by the brute blood of the air,
Did she put on his knowledge with his power
Before the indifferent beak could let her drop?

This is the final version of the sonnet 'Leda and the Swan' as it appears in Yeats's *Collected Poems.* In the early part of this book I have shown that Yeats had an extraordinary variety of interests. Every poem is the result of a complexity of experience. This is borne out by even so short a unit as this sonnet, which is much more than a single idea—it is an idea made up of hundreds of others. ⟨...⟩

What has happened is clear: in 1896 Yeats was thinking of the practices to induce trance states (colours, sounds, odours) as the only possible way to induce some sort of a revelation like the prophecy of re-birth in Virgil's IV Eclogue, but was not very sure of what this revelation would be about; what mattered was to communicate with extra-human powers. By 1925 he thought he knew clearly what to expect: a transformation of the world announced and ushered in by the union of the human with the non-human; since this idea was symbolized in the rape of Leda by the swan, he did not hesitate to mention the myth at this point, and together with it the fall of Troy, referred to in Virgil's IV Eclogue. The words 'another Achilles beleaguer Troy' were removed from a later passage in 'The Adoration of the Magi.' ⟨. . .⟩ They have been transferred here because the new mention of Leda called up in Yeats's mind the fateful event resulting from the union of Leda and the swan. The connecting link between the Leda myth and the fall of Troy is Helen, the offspring of the union of bird and woman. Though mentioned neither in this story nor in the sonnet, Helen, a typically decadent myth, had figured in several other works of Yeats. Even in 'The Adoration of the Magi' the decadent Helen prototype may be felt behind Yeats's description of the dying prostitute in Paris:

> This woman in whose heart all follies have gathered, and in whose body all desires have awaked.

Yeats, in working out his allegory of present decay and future rebirth wanted, in his story, to keep a parallelism with Christian tradition, or rather, an inverted parallelism, since he proposed to show that the new age would be the reversal of the Christian one. He looked, therefore, for the type of woman who would be the exact opposite of the Christian Virgin. As Mr. Ian Fletcher pointed out to me, William Blake described Mary as just such a harlot in this poem 'Was Jesus humble or did he . . . .' But Yeats, living in the *fin de siècle*, chose the fatal woman of the period, the eternal prostitute, the type of Helen-Ennoia described by Flaubert in *La tentation de Saint Antoine.* ⟨. . .⟩

From what has been said we can draw the following conclusions: (1) By 1896 Yeats had already some inkling of the cyclical theory of history which he was later to develop and expound in *A Vision;* (2) The Trojan war, the birth of Christ, and an indefinite event due to happen in our century were already considered by him as three fundamental crises in world history, each of which reversed the established order and ushered in a new cycle of civilization; (3) With the Trojan war he had already associated the figure of Helen, still linked with the decadent conception of the fatal woman, but susceptible of acquiring a more central symbolic significance as the emblem of the first major crisis in civilization (a significance that by

1925 was transferred to the figure of Helen's mother, Leda); (4) The Leda myth, instead, had not particularly impressed Yeats, and became important for him only much later. ⟨...⟩

What brought this fusion about? Why in 1923 did Yeats's 'fancy begin to play with Leda and the swan for metaphor'? The birth of a poem is a sort of sudden and inexplicable release, and the reason why a poem is *poetry* will probably never be satisfactorily explained. But if it is a release, it must be a release of something which already existed in the mind, or if we prefer, in the consciousness, of the creator, the poet. It is the outcome of an immemorial preparatory work, an accumulation of 'materials' which started from the beginning of consciousness (not only individual consciousness, but the consciousness that the individual inherits from the world's past, his culture and his instincts). In other words, each poem has its source in the poet's past experiences, in his reading, in the things he has seen and heard.

—Giorgio Melchiori, *The Whole Mystery of Art: Pattern into Poetry in the Work of W. B. Yeats* (London: Routledge & Kegan Paul, 1960): pp. 73–74, 83–84, 85, 89–90.

PRISCILLA WASHBURN SHAW ON "LEDA AND THE SWAN"

[Priscilla Washburn Shaw is a professor of English and Comparative Literature at the University of California at Santa Cruz. She is the author of *Rilke, Valéry and Yeats: The Domain of the Self*, from which this extract is taken. Here she gives her analysis of the poem.]

The poem does not have the continuity of a story nor the complete presentation of a description; its organization is not a literary reproduction of the organization of external reality, yet it is also not a purely intellectual organization. The action interrupts upon the scene at the beginning with "a sudden blow," and again, in the third stanza, with "a shudder in the loins." It may seem inaccurate to say that a poem begins by an interruption when nothing precedes, but the effect of the opening is just that: It *is* an interruption for the poet. Nor does he stop to explain. We, too, are assumed to be familiar with "the great wings" and "the staggering girl." Or perhaps we also are too struck by the situation to become aware of the more conventional forms of identification such as naming. The exclamations continue, in a series of absolute constructions which give the progression, until the two beings are together. It is not until the last line of the stanza that time is taken for full syntax. After so many details which give only a partial view; which underline the birdlike qualities of the swan; which speak of the girl only in terms of motion, thighs, nape; the repetition of "breast" offers a kind of common denominator, linking the two beings and suggesting something closer to a full picture. Thus, the first bit of action is rounded off and the tempo relaxes with the line: "He holds her helpless breast upon his breast."

With this slowing down of the action, the poet's perspective shifts. The action does not of course stop completely, and the next stanza gives it indirectly in the word "loosening," as in the questions themselves, which could not be asked if the girl's attitude were not changing. But it is clearly subordinated; what is happening is now presented as incidental. The first stanza had stressed the out-thereness of the event; the physical detail was largely external, and none of it attempted to seize the event in its totality, not to present either of the protagonists as a whole. The choice of detail suggested, above all, the movement in the scene and the movement of the eye, as one after another element in the situation attracted attention, and no time was given for a more total perception until the last line.

In the second stanza, on the other hand, we are made aware of the spectator and of the human mind which marvels at the event and tries to grasp and understand it. The shift in tone and perspective is recorded by the opening words "How can . . . ," which are further heightened by their repetition two lines later. At the same time, the stanza represents an attempt to give the inside of the event—for Leda—but in terms which parallel those of the first stanza and yet are still far from the conventional language for depicting emotion. For Yeats continues to spotlight parts of the bodies and to avoid the language of total perception. This technique very appropriately creates an impression of the terrified numbness, the dazed loss of control, and the succumbing to a greater physical force, which is all of Leda's reaction that we are permitted to see. In states of this sort, where it seems emotionally impossible to experience the situation as a whole because of partial shock, there is frequently fixation on detail, so that the stanza seems psychologically accurate as well as metaphorically effective.

But this is not all. In his minimal use of the possessive adjective, and the consequently greater use of somewhat unusual alternative forms, Yeats achieves effects which are curiously suspended between the concrete and the general. Thus, the stanza closes with a question which suggests not only an insight into Leda's reactions, but also some more general rule of human reaction:

> But how can body, laid in that white rush,
> But feel the strange heart beating where it lies?

> (*The Collected Poems*)

The linguistic suggestiveness of the absence of any qualifier for "body" is considerable. It brings to mind the treatment of proper names, and, with it, a touch of personification. At the same time, it echoes analogous treatment of undelimited substances—water, gold, flour—and of abstractions—honesty, life, chastity. (Cf. "Picture and book remain" from "An Acre of Grass" [*The Collected Poems*] for comparable effects.) This merging of the elemental, the abstract, the personal, and the concrete gives the line an unusual extension of meaning, and the same is true to a slightly lesser degree of the phrase "the strange heart," where again the possessive adjective is abandoned in favor of a more general and suggestive form. At the same time, the impact of the syntax is essentially not interrogative. If anything, it would seem that the question form was chosen because of its closeness to the language of exclamation. The effect on the reader is to force assent, to presume corroboration of something which is not totally understood, but which is experienced as overpowering, as precluding alternatives because of its sheer brute strength, and with this the possibility of a genuine question. The two lines really exclaim, "but how could it be otherwise," and this formulation is more emphatic than the conceivable declarative statement, "it could not be otherwise," if only because of the imperious appeal to the reader. There is thus suggested in the language itself an inevitability, which is mental, on the one hand, because it is formulated as a general rule, and real, on the other, because it records the irresistible forward movement of a single external event. We are made simultaneously aware of the reality of both mind and event. The two do not completely fall together; the mind does not reduce the event to an example or pretext, and yet the event does not totally absorb and contain the thought, because the latter is given more general extension than the even it encompasses. This is mind attempting to grasp event, and not, as in Rilke's *Neue Gedichte*, mind subservient to event, the object so completely understood on its own terms that the tension between the mental and the external is no longer visible. That tension is also absent in Valéry, although the nature of the accord that destroys it is different. In Valéry's poetry, the event suits the mind too well, dissolves into it too rapidly, in contrast to Rilke, where precisely the absence of such ready appropriateness leads to a largely single presentation of one or the other side of experience.

We sense in the Yeats the resistance of each to each, of mind to event and event to mind, and this in part because each is allowed its own movement, even while these movements overlap at times. Action will again interrupt the poem "Leda and the Swan," as the reflections of the second stanza are momentarily pushed aside at the beginning of the sestet with a "a shudder in the loins." The lull which permitted reflection is broken with this new impetus from the outside, which then, much as in the opening stanza, leaps past the network of intervening action to the point where the motion subsides into state, and the future can be viewed as present or past. Each of these two stanzas, the first and the third, records the extreme limits of an event, the initial moment of eruption and then the moment at the other end, when the momentum has been dissipated and the effects of the action are spread out and become fully visible. The pattern is that of a projectile, with the focus of interest on the two end points—on the moment of greatest acceleration and then on the moment of stasis in which the motion terminates. The arc which connects these points is traced in the first stanza through the forward rush of the event; in the second, where the compression is even greater, it must be inferred, as the impulse is commuted directly into its result.

The question of the last lines opens the focus of the poem once more and immediately introduces another tempo which is no longer that of the event but of the human mind. As in the second stanza, the thread of the action is still visible through the reflections. The last line, although subordinated to the question, does bring the physical event to a close: "Before the indifferent beak could let her drop." But the focus is clearly elsewhere. The organization no longer suggests the pattern of an external occurrence, for the links are less casual and chronological than logical. The question opens with the reasons for which it is asked, the evidence which will suggest, depending on the interpretation, an affirmative or negative answer. The choice between the two—and it cannot be definitely made— hinges on the principle of reasoning implied: some law of extension or inclusion, or some law of contrasts. In the first case, the stanza asks: Since Leda succumbed to, and experienced so fully, the physical force of the god, did she share as well in his knowledge? The implication is that we might expect from such complete participation in one area, participation in another as well. The question, if so read, is not without a certain wistfulness, which is heightened by the last line with its reference to the "indifferent beak," as well as by the unconcern made explicit in the verb "drop."

—Priscilla Washburn Shaw, *Rilke, Valéry and Yeats: The Domain of the Self*, in *William Butler Yeats*, ed. Harold Bloom (New York: Chelsea House Publishers, 1984): pp. 36–39.

〔ツ〕

THOMAS R. WHITAKER ON THE DIVINE-HUMAN POLAR REALITY

[Thomas R. Whitaker is a professor at Yale University and author of a book on William Carlos Williams (1968), as well as *Mirrors or Our Playing: Paradigms and Presences in Modern Drama* (1999). In this extract taken from his study on Yeats, *Swan and Shadow: Yeats's Dialogue with History* (1964), he discusses the mystery of incarnation.]

That divine-human polar reality at the heart of all power and knowledge, at the unknowable center of the cycles of history, is glimpsed from yet different points of view in other poems. "Leda and the Swan" begins, like "Two Songs from a Play," with overwhelming empathic participation: "A sudden blow: the great wings beating still . . ." After subjecting us to that incursion of a starkly physical power, the octave prolongs the hovering moment of anticipation and moves from direct perception into questions that heighten our awareness of the swan's nature even as they imply the speaker's imperfect apprehension of the event:

> How can those terrified vague fingers push
> The feathered glory from her loosening thighs?
> And how can body, laid in that white rush,
> But feel the strange heart beating where it lies?

Another violent movement carries us into the wider perspective of history:

> A shudder in the loins engenders there
> The broken wall, the burning roof and tower
> And Agamemnon dead.

The alien ecstasy of creation produces—and *is*, proleptically—man's shudder at the violence of destruction. The richly human middle term in that generative series (Helen, Clytemnestra, the Dioscuri) is brutally dropped from view, and the act of generation itself reverberates in the emotional arc of its consequences—"broken wall," "burning . . . tower," and "Agamemnon dead." This moment, in Blake's phrase, "Is equal in its period & value to Six Thousand Years," for

> all the Great
> Events of Time start forth & are conciev'd in such a Period,
> Within a Moment, a Pulsation of the Artery.

Heine had said, "Under Leda's productive hemispheres lay in embryo the whole Trojan world, and you could never understand the far-famed tears of Priam, if I did not first tell you of the ancient eggs of the Swan." But for this speaker, man is less a self-confident creator than a questioning victim:

> Being so caught up,
> So mastered by the brute blood of the air,
> Did she put on his knowledge with his power
> Before the indifferent beak could let her drop?

Postcoital indifference merges with the indifference of that destructively creative power toward the vessels of its impulse, and the climactic question almost answers itself by being asked. The visionary speaker, at least, feels the power that courses through history without being able to understand it.

But may Leda, in suffering a more complete violation than that suffered by this speaker, have been momentarily opened to fuller vision? When the walls are broken, the veils rent, light may flood the soul. The speaker's question therefore points beyond himself toward more completely visionary harlots, fools, and saints. We are left here, however, with the feel of that "strange heart beating" and that still more uncannily autonomous "shudder"—a physical yet more-than-physical spasm that is the source of all life and death. Physical "beating"—of wings or heart or loins—renders, as in "Two Songs from a Play," that violently assaulting mystery of incarnation ("brute blood of the air") which produces all dramas of incarnation.

—Thomas R. Whitaker, *Swan and Shadow: Yeats's Dialogue with History* (Chapel Hill: The University of North Carolina Press, 1964): pp. 107–9.

⊛

RICHARD ELLMANN ON THE RITUALS IN THE POEM

[Richard Ellmann was Goldsmiths' Professor of English at New College, Oxford. He is the foremost scholar of Joyce and Yeats. In this excerpt, taken from his 1964 book *The Identity of Yeats*, he compares different drafts of the poem.]

This account of his rituals has necessarily called attention to the deliberate character of his art. Although he has powerful feelings to express, his poems are in no sense their 'spontaneous overflow.' The 'lyric cry' of Shelley is not his way. He gathers his intensity and force, which have hardly been equalled in modern verse, by creating, with the aid of symbol, myth, and ritual, patterns where thoughts and feelings find unexampled voice. There is nothing unplanned in his art; its many surprises come from long preparation, like the discoveries of a great scientist.

Thus one of his most powerful ritualized moments is the rape of Leda by the swan, but the drafts of his poem about it are evidence that painstaking effort rather than a single flash of inspiration made it possible. If his mind had not constantly dwelled upon the rise and fall of civilizations, upon the 'divine influx' which began each new age, upon Leda as a parallel to Mary because her daughter, like Mary's son, changed the world, upon the terrible consequences of the begetting of Helen, he could never have written the poem. On the other hand, such preoccupations would have come to nothing if he had not decided to focus the poem upon the rape itself, in the description of which he could put all his passion, if he had not been familiar with the myth of Leda in literature and art, and if he had not found contemporary human feeling in the question on which the poem ends, whether power and knowledge can ever be united in life. And even when these elements had been joined, he had to revise again and again before he had submerged them in a completed poem. The first drafts, on which he worked in September 1923, are not vague like the first drafts of his early poems, but they are not sharply focussed:

> Now can the swooping godhead have his will
> Yet hovers, though her helpless thighs are pressed
> By the webbed toes; and that all powerful bill
> Has suddenly bowed her face upon his breast.
> How can those terrified vague fingers push
> The feathered glory from her loosening thighs?
> All the stretched body's laid in that white rush
> And feels the strange heart beating where it lies.
> A shudder in the loins engenders there
> The broken wall, the burning roof and Tower
> And Agamemnon dead. . . .
>   Being so caught up
> Did nothing pass before her in the air?
> Did she put on his knowledge with his power
> Before the indifferent beak could let her drop?

Yeats evidently planned to centre the first quatrain on the god and the second on Leda. Only gradually did she assume more complete dominance of the scene if not of the situation:

> The swooping godhead is half hovering still
> Yet climbs upon her trembling body pressed
> By the webbed toes; and that all powerful bill
> Has suddenly bowed her face upon his breast.

> The swooping godhead is half hovering still
> But mounts, until her trembling thighs are pressed
> By the webbed toes, and that all powerful bill
> Can hold her helpless body on his breast.

> How can those terrified vague fingers push
> The feathered glory from her loosening thighs?
> All the stretched body's laid on that white rush
> And feels the strange heart beating where it lies.
> A shudder in the loins engenders there
> The broken wall, the burning roof and tower
> And Agamemnon dead.
>
>   Being mounted so
> So mastered by the brute blood of the air,
> Did she put on his knowledge with his power
> Before the indifferent beak could let her go?

Gradually the opening syntax became strained to give more dramatic shock:

> A swoop upon great wings and hovering still
> The bird descends, and her frail thighs are pressed
>
> A rush, a sudden wheel and hovering still. . . .

When the poem was first published in an ill-fated review, *To-Morrow*, in August 1924, Yeats had still not got the first lines as he wanted them:

> A rush, a sudden wheel, and hovering still
> The bird descends, and her frail thighs are pressed
> By the webbed toes, and that all-powerful bill
> Has laid her helpless face upon his breast.
> How can those terrified vague fingers push
> The feathered glory from her loosening thighs!
> All the stretched body's laid on the white rush
> And feels the strange heart beating where it lies;
> A shudder in the loins engenders there
> The broken wall, the burning roof and tower
> And Agamemnon dead.
>
>   Being so caught up,
> So mastered by the brute blood of the air,
> Did she put on his knowledge with his power
> Before the indifferent beak could let her drop?

But by 1925, in *A Vision*, he had at least brought the octave to the same perfection as the sestet:

> A sudden blow: the great wings beating still
> Above the staggering girl, her thighs caressed
> By the dark webs, her nape caught in his bill,
> He holds her helpless breast upon his breast.
> How can those terrified vague fingers push
> The feathered glory from her loosening thighs?

And how can body, laid in that white rush,
But feel the strange heart beating where it lies?
A shudder in the loins engenders there
The broken wall, the burning roof and tower
And Agamemnon dead.
                    Being so caught up,
So mastered by the brute blood of the air,
Did she put on his knowledge with his power
Before the indifferent beak could let her drop?

The scene was now realized without the sacrifice of any of its implications for him. The new beginning lent an air of inevitability and destiny to the god's descent; the historical results of the ritualistic begetting were epitomized in the images, at once physical and remote, of the beginning of the sestet; and the personal, contemporary problem emerged in the final lines. The example gives evidence that to talk about Yeats's rituals, myths, and symbols, is to talk about his passions and ideas, in fact his whole being.

'I always feel,' Yeats wrote to Sturge Moore, 'that my work is not drama but the ritual of a lost faith.' It is so in that it constantly returns to the past for support, but without slavishness, for it alters the past even as it re-creates it. The world of letters divides itself more and more readily in our time into those who regard the forms of life as ceaselessly changing and those who regard them as a series of repetitions or recurrences. Yeats sides vigorously with ritual rather than with helter-skelter change.

—Richard Ellmann, *The Identity of Yeats* (New York: Oxford University Press, 1964): pp. 176–79.

⊛

WILLIAM H. O'DONNELL ON THE POEM'S EMPHASIS ON PHYSICALITY

[William H. O'Donnell is the author of *The Poetry of William Butler Yeats*, from which this extract is taken. Here he explains the technical success of the poem.]

The poems of *The Tower* record many acts of violence, and surely one of the most horrific of them is the bestial violation of Leda.

"Leda and the Swan" pays avid, even leering attention to the explicit physical details of that savage mythic event, and yet, for some sixty years, the poem has fascinated rather than offended its readers—of both sexes.

To understand how "Leda and the Swan" can arouse fascination rather than offense, the reader needs to recall that the rape of Leda may be considered in several ways. On the immediate physical level it is a bizarre sexual incident of which the reader is a poetical voyeur. More abstractly, the rape could be an emblem of the violence of the Irish Civil War of 1922–23; the poem is often published with its date, 1923, perhaps to draw attention to those troubled times. More abstractly still, in Yeats's theory of history the rape of Leda fits into a recurring series of annunciations.

Yeats printed "Leda and the Swan" as an introductory poem to the "Dove or Swan" section of *A Vision*, where he discusses his cyclical theory of history. In it, the rape of Leda fits into a series of brief but key moments in history when god and mortal intersect. These encounters, which happen only once in each two-thousand-year cycle of history, produce the avatar of the next cycle. The swan is here the messenger of a pagan annunciation, just as the dove, representing the Holy Ghost, attends the Christian annunciation. For Yeats, the violence that is so prominent in "Leda and the Swan" is also part of the parallelism between Leda and the Virgin Mary, as he shows in the poem "Wisdom," which he once intended to place immediately before "Leda and the Swan." "Wisdom" mentions the Virgin Mary's "horror" and Christ's "wild infancy." A later poem, "A Nativity" (1938), describes Mary as "terror-struck." Leda and Mary each, if only briefly, had physical contact with an immortal and therefore each resembles, to some degree, a magus or a mystic who gains access to the supernatural wisdom of God. This was another reason for Yeats's fascination with the myth of Leda.

The rape of Leda is, of course, also distanced from ordinary experience by being mythical. In nearly all the principal versions of this legend, Zeus is attracted to the mortal Leda by her great beauty and seduces her in the form of a swan. The offspring of that seduction include at least Helen of Troy. Other versions expand the list of children, first by including the immortal Pollux (Polydeuces) and then by adding his twin brother Castor and, more rarely, Clytemnestra, who became the wife of Agamemnon. In *A Vision*

(1925), which includes this poem, Yeats mentioned two of Leda's eggs, from which came "Love" and "War." He also noted that an "unhatched" egg of hers was displayed as a holy relic in a Spartan temple.

Most accounts of this myth describe Zeus's action in polite euphemisms such as "visited" or "seduced." But the action of the myth is sexual and shares the explicitly physical overtones of Zeus's encounter with Europa, when he took the form of a bull. It does not use the remote symbolism of a shower of gold, the form in which he seduced Danae and fathered Perseus. Yeats's focus on the physical details of the rape is therefore available in the myth, even if his decision to give them such vigorous prominence in the poem might well be evidence that he had begun rehearsing his later role as the "Wild Wicked Old Man" of a 1938 poem.

The six successive drafts of the opening line demonstrate an increasingly explicit focus on the physical violence of the rape. Yeats's first version was predominantly narrative rather than graphic:

> Now can the swooping godhead have his will.

An intermediate version concentrated on the physical action without first establishing the context:

> A swoop upon great wings and hovering still.

And then the final version carries that focus on violence even further by replacing "swoop" with "sudden blow." It adds emphasis by breaking the rhythms of the first line into two halves, with an explosive opening and an immediate halt before the line continues: "A sudden blow: the great wings beating still." The poem pays careful attention to physical details of "the staggering girl"—"thighs caressed," "helpless breast," "loosening thighs" and the "shudder in the loins"—and to sexual details like the postcoital lassitude of Zeus, mentioned in the final line ("the indifferent beak could let her drop").

Even if the sexual brutality and directness of this brief poem are set aside, its diction is sufficiently violent to permit it to contribute an ample share to *The Tower*'s evocation of the Irish Civil War's savagery: "sudden blow," "staggering," "caught," "helpless," "terrified," "shudder," "broken," "burning," "dead," and "brute blood."

The technical success of this poem, with its extraordinarily skillful manipulation of language also deserves notice. A brief list of the fine effects of diction would include the pun on "still" in the first line and the startling contrast between the pleasurable sensuousness of "her thighs caressed" and the grotesque "dark webs." Rhythmic triumphs can be found in the cacophonous violence of "shudder," which is followed by a contrasting, smoothly flowing line 10, "The broken wall, the burning roof and tower," and then the majestic slowing to a full stop in midline: "And Agamemnon dead." This broken half-line and the stanza division between lines 4 and 5 only partially disguise this fourteen-line, iambic pentameter poem's near use of the Italian sonnet form.

The final question asked—"Did she put on his knowledge with his power?"—lends an aura of mystery, despite the speculation by scholars of *A Vision* who think that Leda probably had only physical contact with Zeus, and that she did not acquire any divine wisdom before the indifferent beak could let her drop. The open question gives the poem some resonance, but does not altogether set aside an overwhelming emphasis on physicality.

—William H. O'Donnell, *The Poetry of William Butler Yeats* (New York: Ungar, 1986): pp. 99–102.

Thematic Analysis of
"Sailing to Byzantium"

Yeats wrote this poem in the autumn of 1926, and by placing it at the opening of his finest single volume of poems, *The Tower*, he gave it special prominence.

Trying to explain the poem, Yeats wrote a comment for a BBC broadcast in September 1931:

> Now I am trying to write about the state of my soul, for it is right for an old man to make his soul, and some of my thoughts upon that subject I have put into a poem called "Sailing to Byzantium." When Irishmen were illuminating the Book of Kells [in the eighth century] and making the jeweled croziers in the National Museum, Byzantium was a centre of European civilization and the source of its spiritual philosophy, so I symbolize the search for the spiritual life by a journey to that city.

The first stanza opens urgently:

> That is no country for old men. The young
> In one another's arms, birds in the trees

It is revealing that as late as 1937, Yeats was willing to change the opening lines for ease of reading into:

> Old men should quit a country where the young
> In one another's arms; birds in the trees

Fortunately, he did not.

The poet leaves behind "those dying generations" and sails to "the holy city of Byzantium," identifying himself in his old age as "a paltry thing, / A tattered coat upon a stick."

The persona of the poem seeks out the city that Yeats described in *A Vision* as the one place he would choose to live if he were given a month to spend in Antiquity: "In early Byzantium, maybe never before or since in recorded history, religious, aesthetic, and practical life were one." At first Yeats tried to illustrate his quest for enlightenment with the concrete aspects of Byzantium, as his early drafts of the poem show. However, by the last version Yeats had replaced those aspects with symbolic portrayals of the city. In the poem's final rendering, Byzantium certainly loses its primary meaning, as some critics have justly seen it, and begins to stand for a holy city of Yeats's imagination, as Golgonooza did for William Blake.

Much speculation has been uttered on the subject of the origin of the bird in the last stanza.

> Once out of nature I shall never take
> My bodily form from any natural thing,
> But such a form as Grecian goldsmiths make
> Of hammered gold and gold enameling
> To keep a drowsy Emperor awake;
> Or set upon a golden bough to sing
> To lords and ladies of Byzantium
> Of what is past, or passing, or to come.

The golden bird's song reveals the past, present, and future to the lords and ladies of Byzantium. The bird may represent the poet's soul and passionate heart. Yeats's remark on this topic doesn't help us much in our interpretation. The note reads: "I have read somewhere that in the Emperor's palace at Byzantium was a tree made of gold and silver, and artificial birds that sang." It may be best to agree with Jon Stallworthy, who sensibly advises that Yeats deliberately does not specify the nature of his golden bird and that we should resist the temptation to do so for him. Many other critics have identified the bird as an echo of Keats's or Shelley's nightingale, or even that of Hans Christian Andersen in his tale "The Emperor's Nightingale."

The poem closes with the line "past, passing, or to come," which echoes the sixth line of the first stanza: "Whatever is begotten, born, and dies." It also brings to mind the first two lines of Blake's "Introduction" to *Songs of Experience*: "Hear the voice of the Bard! / Who Present, Past, & Future sees."

This poem came out of a mood of despair at the coming of old age, and is packed tight with philosophical and historical thought. Perhaps the test of the poem's strength is whether it works without applying the apparatus of *A Vision*, or bending it to the use of scholars who hope to untangle some of Yeats's complex and unorthodox ideas. The poem's seemingly precise references are truly boundless in their suggestiveness of meditation on youth, age, and death. Most critics—and readers—agree that the poem is admirably strong on its own merits. ❀

Critical Views on
"Sailing to Byzantium"

CLEANTH BROOKS ON "SAILING TO BYZANTIUM" AS A
METAPHYSICAL POEM

[Cleanth Brooks (1906–1975), the notable critic of the New
Criticism, was Gray Professor of Rhetoric at Yale University
from 1947 to 1975. He published two textbooks with
Robert Penn Warren, *Understanding Poetry* (1938) and
Understanding Fiction (1943). This extract is taken from
his book *Modern Poetry and the Tradition*. Here he
discusses the richness of Yeats's symbolism.]

Yeats's symbols are, after all, nothing but concrete and meaningful
images in terms of which the play of the mind may exhibit itself—
that play being, not rigidly conceptual and bare, but enriched with
all sorts of associations. Yeats's later poetry, like the poetry of Donne,
reveals the "mind at the finger-tips."

Consider, for example, his "Sailing to Byzantium." If we follow the
poem carefully, we shall be able to detect even the syllogistic
framework which characterizes so much of metaphysical poetry. The
poet reasons as follows: His country is a land of natural beauty,
beauty of the body. But his own body is old. The soul must,
therefore, sing the louder to compensate for the old and dying flesh.

> An aged man is but a paltry thing,
> A tattered coat upon a stick, unless
> Soul clap its hands and sing, and louder sing
> For every tatter in its mortal dress.

But there is no singing school for the soul except in studying the
works of the soul. "And therefore" he has sailed to Byzantium, for
the artists of Byzantium do not follow the forms of nature but
intellectual forms, ideal patterns. He appeals to them to

> Consume my heart away; sick with desire
> And fastened to a dying animal

and by severing him from the dying world of the body, to gather him
into what is at least "the artifice of eternity."

Once out of nature I shall never take
My bodily form from any natural thing,
But such a form as Grecian goldsmiths make
Of hammered gold and gold enamelling
To keep a drowsy Emperor awake;
Or set upon a golden bough to sing
To lords and ladies of Byzantium
Of what is past, or passing, or to come.

A comparison of this paraphrase with the poem in its entirety illustrates better than anything else why the poet must write as he does—how much we lose by substituting abstract statements for his richer "symbols." Byzantium is, for instance, a very rich symbol. It may be thought a very indefinite one. But richness and complexity are not vagueness, and it will be easy to show that the symbol has its precision. It means many things, but if one misses the connection with the intellectual art, one has missed the poem. (Some of the further things which it means may be best deferred to Chapter VIII, where we shall consider Yeats's poetry in relation to his system of esoteric beliefs.)

The images, for the most part, are not especially unpoetic. The average reader will balk, not so much at the images as at the amount of intellectual exercise demanded of him. And yet one observes that the poet has the soul perform in a more unconventional manner ("clap hands and sing") than most Victorians would have permitted; and that Yeats has brought a scarecrow and the "lords and ladies of Byzantium" into close and successful fusion. There is irony and wit—serious wit—in a phrase like "the artifice of eternity." Indeed, the fantasy and extravagance of the poem would cause one to call it, in Wordsworth's terms, a poem of the fancy as opposed to the imagination, except that it has a tragic seriousness which has nothing to do with the playful fancy of Wordsworth. And this is perhaps the surest mark of all that here we have a case of symbolist poetry becoming metaphysical. ⟨. . .⟩

"Sailing to Byzantium" is a metaphysical poem quite as much as it is a symbolist poem. We may prefer to use the former term when we are thinking primarily of the assimilation of diverse materials which it accomplishes; the latter term, when we are thinking primarily of the mode of its statement as opposed to that of "scientific" prose— the use of image rather than abstract concept. But such a distinction (I have no enthusiasm for it) is merely one of convenience and points to two different aspects of a poetry which are not mutually exclusive, and which are both basic to the poetic method. They are not only not mutually exclusive—they tend to occur together.

—Cleanth Brooks, *Modern Poetry and the Tradition* (Chapel Hill: University of North Carolina Press, 1939): pp. 62–64, 64–65.

⊗

GIORGIO MELCHIORI ON THE VISUAL ORIGIN OF THE POEM

[Giorgio Melchiori is the author of *Joyce in Rome: The Genesis of Ulysses* (1984). His most recent work is *Italian Studies in Shakespeare and His Contemporaries* (1999). This extract is taken from his book *The Whole Mystery of Art*. Here he asserts that the origin of "Sailing to Byzantium" is visual.]

One more fact should be kept in mind: the two poems were written at a distance of four years: 'Sailing to Byzantium' in August–September 1926, 'Byzantium' between April and September 1930. The first was written (concurrently with 'Among School Children') 'to recover *his* spirits,' and the second to 'warm *him*self back into life' after an illness, and 'looking for a theme that might befit *his* years.'

These points are not trivial, especially in view of the attempts of recent critics to demonstrate that the subject matter of the two poems is somewhat different and suggests a shift in the attitude of the author. 'Sailing,' they find, describes the search for the 'country of the mind,' while 'Byzantium' proper is a presentation of an ideal state beyond life. The distinction finds support in the fact that—as F. L. Gwynn pointed out—the Byzantium of the first poem is that of about A.D. 550, the period mentioned in the famous description in *A Vision* 'a little before Justinian opened St. Sophia and closed the Academy of Plato'; while in the second poem it is that of about A.D. 1000 'towards the end of the first Christian millenium,' as Yeats stated in the note of 30 April 1930, his first mention of an idea for his second poem. ⟨. . .⟩

The strictly visual inspiration of the first draft should be noted: Yeats obviously began with two pictures in his mind's eye—a

Renaissance Madonna expressing the humanization of the supernatural, the fullness of *earthly* life, and the stylized splendour of Byzantine mosaics and architectural forms which symbolize in a direct way the supernatural itself, the fullness of life beyond the boundaries of earth and flesh. The origin of 'Sailing to Byzantium' is visual, it is symbolic painting. But in revising it Yeats completely blotted out the two pictures as such, and was content to leave only indirect suggestions of them. This transformation shows how deeply he was conscious of his medium of expression: the sensuousness of poetry lies not in its descriptiveness but in the thought.

In the earliest draft the poem began:

> All in this land—my Maker that is play
> Or else asleep upon His Mother's knees,

and this was revised with a further stress on the Madonna painting:

> Here all is young; the chapel walls display
> An infant sleeping on his Mother's knees,

It is a far cry from this to the final form of the poem:

> That is no country for old men. The young
> In one another's arms, birds in the trees— ⟨. . .⟩

Keats, in the 'Ode to a Nightingale'—which, as Dr. Tillyard has noticed, is echoed by Yeats in 'Sailing to Byzantium'—and Shelley in a passage of 'Rosalind and Helen' that Yeats himself quoted at length in his essay on Shelley, evoke eternity through the image of the nightingale. The solitary bird and its song stand for aesthetic beauty, the beauty of art, but also for that of nature. In Yeats the nightingale becomes an artificial golden bird, as he says in 'Sailing':

> Once out of nature I shall never take
> My bodily form from any natural thing,
> But such a form as Grecian goldsmiths make
> Of hammered gold and gold enamelling
> To keep a drowsy Emperor awake;
> Or set upon a golden bough to sing
> To lords and ladies of Byzantium
> Of what is past, or passing, or to come.

Nature is rejected, and the poet shows how faithful he has remained to the doctrine of art for art's sake current in his youth. While in Keats and Shelley art was represented by music, by the song of the bird, Yeats instead is thinking mainly in terms of the visual arts. What matters is not so much the bird's song, but that the bird is artificial, an artefact. It is a work of plastic art which scorns 'aloud / In glory of changeless metal / Common bird or petal / And all complexities of mire or blood.'

> —Giorgio Melchiori, *The Whole Mystery of Art: Pattern into Poetry in the Work of W. B. Yeats* (London: Routledge & Kegan Paul, 1960): pp. 201–2, 202–3, 209–11.

֍

CURTIS B. BRADFORD ON THE BACKGROUND OF THE POEM

[Curtis B. Bradford is the author or editor of several books on Yeats, among them *Yeats at Work* (1965) and *W. B. Yeats: The Writing of the Player Queen* (1977). This extract is taken from his essay "Yeats's Byzantium Poems: A Study of Their Development." Here he discusses the background of the poem.]

Yeats's interest in Byzantine art and civilization began in the Nineties and continued through his life. The first issue of "Rosa Alchemica" (1896) refers to the mosaic work at Ravenna ("mosaic not less beautiful than the mosaic in the Baptistery at Ravenna, but of a less severe beauty"), work which Yeats probably saw when in 1907 he travelled in Italy with Lady Gregory. Unfortunately, Yeats has left us no account of his visit to Ravenna. A revision of "The Holy Places," final section of *Discoveries,* made for the 1912 edition of *The Cutting of an Agate,* shows that between 1906 and 1912 Yeats's knowledge of Byzantine history had increased. In 1906 he wrote of "an unstable equilibrium of the whole European mind that would not have come had Constantinople wall been built of better stone"; in 1912 this became "had John Palaeologus cherished, despite that high and heady look . . . a hearty disposition to fight the Turk." In preparation for the "Dove or Swan" section of *A Vision,* which Yeats finished at Capri in February 1925, and left virtually unchanged in the revised *A Vision* of 1937, Yeats read several books about Byzantine art and civilization and studied Byzantine mosaics in Rome and Sicily. He did not return to Ravenna, being fearful of its miasmal air. Once Byzantium had found a place in "the System," it shortly appeared in the poetry, first in "Sailing to Byzantium," and "Wisdom" (1926–27); then changed, though not utterly, in "Byzantium" (1930).

From his reading and, especially, from his experience of Byzantine art Yeats constructed Byzantium, his golden city of the imagination. The Byzantium to which we travel in "Sailing to Byzantium" is Justinian's city as Yeats described it in "Dove or Swan," an imagined land where Unity of Being has permeated an entire culture. Yeats wrote three comments on this poem in a manuscript book and two radio speeches.

The comment in the manuscript book is part of an account of a séance Yeats had with a London medium, Mrs. Cooper. Since Yeats wrote a longer and already published account of a "book test" which was part of this séance (in a letter to Olivia Shakespear dated 27 October), I quote only a suggestive comment somewhat different from the comment made in the letter: "I had just finished a poem in which a poet of the Middle Ages besought the saints 'in the holy fire' to send their ecstasy." (Transcribed from the manuscript book begun at Oxford, 7 April 1921). The remark about "a poet of the Middle Ages" reminds us that the "I persona" in a poem by Yeats is sometimes a dramatization, Yeats, that is, in a mask assumed for the duration of a poem. A knowledge of Yeats's intention here will help us to understand the successive drafts of the poem. In the early drafts Yeats is consciously medievalizing; the "poet of the Middle Ages" gradually disappears until the action of the finished poem is timeless, recurrent, eternal.

The second comment was intended for a reading Yeats made from his poems over the BBC, Belfast, 8 September 1931. Yeats omitted both text and comment from the final script:

> Now I am trying to write about the state of my soul, for it is right for an old man to make his soul, and some of my thoughts upon that subject I have put into a poem called "Sailing to Byzantium." When Irishmen were illuminating the Book of Kells and making the jewelled croziers in the National Museum, Byzantium was the center of European civilization and the source of its spiritual philosophy, so I symbolize the search for the spiritual life by a journey to that city.

The third comment occurred in the broadcast "My Own Poetry," given from London, 3 July 1937. It concerns the golden bird:

I speak of a bird made by Grecian goldsmiths. There is a record of a tree of gold with artificial birds which sang. The tree was somewhere in the Royal Palace of Byzantium. I use it as a symbol of the intellectual joy of eternity, as contrasted with the instinctive joy of human life.

The central correlative of "Byzantium" is not Justinian's sixth century city. The prose version of the poem makes this clear. I give that as Yeats first wrote it, with a long cancelled passage.

Subject for a poem

Describe Byzantium as it is in the system towards the end of the first Christian millennium. (The worn ascetics on the walls contrasted with their [?] splendour. A walking mummy. A spiritual refinement and perfection amid a rigid world. A sigh of wind—autumn leaves in the streets. The divine born amidst natural decay.)

In ink of a different color, hence presumably at a later time, Yeats cancelled the passage I have placed in parentheses, and wrote over it:

. . . A walking mummy; flames at the street corners where the soul is purified. Birds of hammered gold singing in the golden trees. In the harbour [dolphins] offering their backs to the wailing dead that they may carry them to paradise. [Both passages transcribed from the MS of the 1930 Diary.]

When we look in *A Vision* for a description of Byzantium near the end of the tenth century, we do not easily find it. Perhaps Yeats had in mind the concluding paragraphs of section IV of "Dove or Swan," perhaps he is there describing both Eastern and Western Europe. The thought of those paragraphs is similar to the thought of the original prose version of "Byzantium," quoted above, especially in this passage:

. . . All that is necessary to salvation is known, but as I conceive the age there is much apathy. Man awaits death and judgment with nothing to occupy the worldly faculties and is helpless before the world's disorder, and this may have dragged up out of the subconscious the conviction that the world was about to end. Hidden, except at rare moments of excitement or revelation, and even then shown but in symbol, the stream of *recurrence,* set in motion by the Galilean Symbol, has filled its basin, and seems motionless for an instant before it falls over the rim. . . . [*A Vision*, 1924.]

In this later Byzantium Unity of Being is threatened, though it is miraculously restored when the symbolic dolphins carry the souls of the dead to a Yeatsean paradise, a paradise of art, art which is at once sensual and spiritual. Yeats makes this interpretation of "Byzantium" in a passage cancelled from the MS of his unpublished lecture "Modern Ireland," written for his final American lecture tour of 1932-33. He has been writing of O'Leary, to whom he has ascribed Aristotle's "magnificence." He then stops to comment on "magnificence."

> Aristotle says that if you give a ball to [a] child, and if it was the best ball in the market, though it cost but sixpence, it is an example of magnificence: and style, whether in life or literature, comes, I think, from excess, from that something over and above utility which wrings the heart. (In my later poems I have called it Byzantium, that city where the saints showed their wasted forms upon a background of gold mosaic, and an artificial bird sang upon a tree of gold in the presence of the emperor; and in one poem I have pictured the ghosts swimming, mounted upon dolphins, through the sensual seas, that they may dance upon its pavements.) [Transcribed from the MS. I have placed the cancelled passage in parentheses.]

This comment, taken together with the fact that Byzantine art works break the flood of images, the bitter furies of complexity at the climax of "Byzantium," indicates that Yeats's later Byzantium, though he distinguishes it from his earlier, remains essentially the same. This sameness in difference is a characteristic stratagem with Yeats. In the development of nearly all his recurring symbols new shades of meaning will be added while the old meanings are retained.

—Curtis B. Bradford, "Yeats's Byzantium Poems: A Study of Their Development," in *Yeats: A Collection of Critical Essays,* ed. John Unterecker (Englewood Cliffs, N.J.: Prentice Hall, 1963): pp. 93–96.

⊕

THOMAS R. WHITAKER ON "SAILING TO BYZANTIUM"

[Thomas R. Whitaker is a professor at Yale University and author of a book on William Carlos Williams (1968), as well as *Mirrors or Our Playing: Paradigms and Presences in Modern Drama* (1999). In this extract taken from his study

on Yeats, *Swan and Shadow: Yeats's Dialogue with History*
(1964), he talks about Yeats's alchemical goal.]

⟨T⟩he Plotinian journey of "Sailing to Byzantium" is completed only in aspiration. The poem hints at the alchemical goal, the quintessence or "bird born out of the fire," a stone—"hammered gold and gold enamelling"—placed so firmly in a living world that it contains the ironies of the "terrible beauty" of "Easter 1916." Significantly, however, that stone is not dumb, troubling the living with memories of a past moment; it sings of "what is past, or passing, or to come." It is no sleepy mystery; though unliving, it is more lively than its drowsy Byzantine setting. But it is not more alive than the richly passionate speaker, who endows with vitality both sensual music and purgation by fire. And that irony stresses the fact that finally the speaker is his own bird—a "living philosophical stone," in Robert Flood's phrase—soul clapping its hands and singing in its own "artifice of eternity." He has changed, in a moment, but still sings of time.

Reworking Blake's doctrine of "self-annihilation," fusing in one instant what Schopenhauer called the "will, of which life is the mirror, and knowledge free from the will, which beholds it clearly in that mirror," Yeats could find history transcended in an eternal moment of striving and contemplation. So the subjective tragedians Dante and Villon had found it, he thought: and "we gaze at such men in awe, because we gaze not at a work of art, but at the re-creation of the man through that art, the birth of a new species of man . . ." Attempting like them to "live for contemplation" and yet keep his "intensity," Yeats discovered his tragic stone in such poems as "Sailing to Byzantium" and "Among School Children." In them is created a new species of man who—unbeknownst to himself, as it were—*is* his contrary, and so, though "mirrored in all the suffering of desire," would not change his luck. Hence the piercing vigor, even exultation, in the conclusions of such poems, where expression of desire is at the same time ecstasy in the attainment of the true goal.

—Thomas R. Whitaker, *Swan and Shadow: Yeats's Dialogue with History* (Chapel Hill: The University of North Carolina Press, 1964): pp. 274–75.

☙

[Richard Ellmann was Goldsmiths' Professor of English at New College, Oxford. He is the foremost scholar of Joyce and Yeats. This excerpt is taken from his book *The Identity of Yeats*. Here he discusses the origin of the ambivalence in the poem.]

Important as *A Vision* is, it is in no sense a complete guide-book to Yeats's poetry. It provides him with a valuable system of symbols, but the attempt to interpret any poem solely in terms of the system will do it an injustice. Yeats was quite willing to hold *A Vision* in abeyance if his experience dictated some attitude not to be found in it. We need not wonder that, in spite of his promise in the book that the next era would be subjective and preferable to the present, the god of that era, who rises from the desert sands in the poem 'The Second Coming,' is no beneficent Dionysus but a monster. The poet's vision of horror surmounts his vision of the cycles. In the same way, his prose statements about Byzantium give no indication of the ambivalence to be found in 'Sailing to Byzantium.' No one would suppose, on reading the extra-national *Vision,* that Ireland would occur so prominently in the poetry written contemporaneously with it; nor would anyone expect that the saint, who stands near the 'objective' dark of the moon, would receive such favourable consideration in 'The Gyres.'

A Vision is not, then, a full background for his verse; it is drawn upon when it is needed, sometimes running counter to the verse, sometimes parallel, sometimes compounding with it. In verse, as in prose, Yeats was searching to find adequate expression for the contest of self and soul, and the transcendence or equilibration of this contest. His winding stair, which suggests the tortuous path of life, has a tower around it to suggest fixity; these symbols are parallel to the gyres and sphere, and priority is impossible to assign. Both themes have to be given play. He has many ways of representing the contest: he sets self against soul directly in 'A Dialogue of Self and Soul,' more concretely in the encounters of Crazy Jane and the Bishop, or in the tree of 'Vacillation' which is half green leaf and half burning flame. That tree is comparable to Yeats's old tree of life, but both sides of the tree have been shot through with energy since 'The

Two Trees.' He puts the conflict also in 'Sailing to Byzantium,' more bluntly in an early draft than in the completed poem:

Fish, flesh & fowl, all spring & summer long
Extol what is begotten, born, & dies
And man has made no monument to extol
The unborn, undying unbegotten soul.

The contest is less ultimate than it appears: Crazy Jane is no atheist; she merely finds all the religious terms applicable to physical union and human love. According to her lights, she is more truly religious than the pompous bishop, just as the self in the 'Dialogue' is more truly blessed in the end than the soul, and the poet in 'Sailing to Byzantium' is not less interested in life but more capable of regarding it once he has been transformed into a singing bird. There is always a means of escape from the prison of the antinomies, though it is not always grasped.

—Richard Ellmann, *The Identity of Yeats* (New York: Oxford University Press, 1964): pp. 164–66.

73

Thematic Analysis of
"Byzantium"

Generally the most admired of Yeats's poems, "Byzantium" is considered one of the most complex. It was written in 1930, four years after "Sailing to Byzantium." If we are to believe Yeats, he wrote it "to warm himself back to life." The poem originated in response to the objection his friend Sturge Moore voiced about "Sailing to Byzantium." Moore wrote to Yeats that "Sailing to Byzantium" had let him down in the fourth stanza, "as such a goldsmith's bird is as much nature as a man's body, especially if it only sings like Homer and Shakespeare of what is past or passing or to come to Lords and Ladies." That remark helped Yeats realize "that the idea needed exposition."

The initial prose draft of "Byzantium" lists the subjects mentioned in the poem:

> Subject for a poem. Death of a friend . . . Describe Byzantium as it is in the system [explained in *A Vision*] towards the end of the first millennium. A walking mummy; flames at the street corners where the soul is purified. Birds of hammered gold singing in the golden trees. In the harbour (dolphins) offering their backs to the wailing dead that they may carry them to Paradise. These subjects have been in my head for some time, especially the last.

The poem is written in the rhyme scheme AA BB CDDC, which Yeats had already used in "Memory of Major Robert Gregory" and "A Prayer for My Daughter."

This curiously subtle poem, full of meanings, opens with images that bear strong resemblance to Blake's poem "London":

> The unpurged images of day recede;
> The Emperor's drunken soldiery are abed;
> Night resonance recedes, night-walker's song
> After great cathedral gong;
> A starlit or a moonlit dome disdains
> All that man is,
> All mere complexities,
> The fury and the mire of human veins.

Similar images, such as "soldier," "palace," "midnight street," and "harlot's curse" previously appeared in Blake's lyric:

And the hapless Soldier's sigh
Runs in blood down Palace walls.

But most thro' midnight streets I hear
How the youthful Harlot's curse
Blasts the new-born infant's tear,

The "starlit or moonlit dome" cited in the first stanza may reflect Yeats's fascination with the waxing and waning of the moon. In *A Vision*, the 28 phases of the moon are considered to represent the phases of human mind and human civilization; these phases play a significant role in Yeats's philosophical system.

The movement of "Byzantium" proceeds from when "the unpurged images of day recede" to "midnight," when the ghostly guide emerges. Besides a strong suggestion of a narrative that is hard to decipher, the poem also indicates spatial movement through the streets of the city to the sea, where dolphins deliver spirits to the afterlife.

The poet's persona enters the poem in the second stanza. He sees an image, either in a state of trance or transcendence, of a "man or shade," then utters a wonderfully inventive phrase: "Shade more than man, more image than a shade." In the last line of the second stanza, "I call it death-in-life and life-in-death," the critics have found a Coleridgean image, from the *Rime of the Ancient Mariner*: "The nightmare Life-in-Death was she, / Who thicks man's blood with cold." At the end of the stanza, the poet hails the superhuman image, reminding us of Dante and his guide through the valley of death in *The Inferno*.

Next evoked is a golden bird who definitely must bear some relationship to the golden birds of "Sailing to Byzantium." Critics still argue about its function.

The five stanzas of the poem are somehow disconnected, and the delicate connections between them are vague. The fifth stanza skillfully gathers phrases from the previous stanzas, achieving the fullness of verbal music, but we feel the poet's control over images and wording perhaps too much. This provides further evidence of the truth of what Yeats himself said in a letter to Fiora Macleod: "I do so much of my work by the critical, rather than the imaginative quality."

Astraddle on the dolphin's mire and blood,
Spirit after spirit! The smithies break the flood.
The golden smithies of the Emperor!
Marbles of the dancing floor
Break bitter furies of complexity,
Those images that yet
Fresh images beget,
That dolphin-torn, that gong-tormented sea.

Some of the questions the poem raises—still under critical debate—are: What is Yeats's greatest poetic strength in this poem? What are the poem's limitations compared to its success, besides its extraordinarily successful phrasing?

We may find useful consolation in the words of Jon Stallworthy, who said: "No matter from what angle one approaches Yeats's 'Byzantium,' and many critics have traveled by many different routes, its magic and mystery defy definition, and at every point one is aware of other levels and areas of meaning, still unexplored, just beyond the range of sight."

In the poem's closely knit unity, full of atmospheric and evocative power, the ultimate meaning cannot be spelled out. The poem, with its considerable though uneven strength, succeeds largely because the reader is taken under its calculated spell and then allowed to take his or her own meanings from it. ❀

Critical Views on
"Byzantium"

G. WILSON KNIGHT ON THE POETICAL CONTEXT OF THE
IMAGERY OF "BYZANTIUM"

[G. Wilson Knight (1897–1985), a leading British
Shakespearean scholar, taught drama and English literature
at the University of Leeds. He was the author of many
volumes of criticism, including *The Wheel of Fire* (1930),
The Starlit Dome (1941), *The Crown of Life* (1947), and
Shakespeare and Religion (1967). In this extract, taken from
The Starlit Dome, he explores the relationship between
Yeats's imagery and that of previous poets.]

Yeats's *Sailing to Byzantium* contrasts the 'sensual music' of young
love, trees and water-life, all existence, we are told, *within the birth-
death enclosure*, with 'monuments of unageing intellect' and artistic
wisdom. Having sailed the 'seas' to the 'holy city of Byzantium' he
prays sages standing in 'God's holy fire' as in 'the gold mosaic of a
wall' to gather him 'into the *artifice* of eternity.' The symbolism is
deliberately metallic, almost brittle, and ends by imaging life beyond
nature as golden birds (like the miracle-bird in *Zapolya*) singing of
past, present, and future to amuse a Byzantine Emperor. This
'emperor' is all but 'God.' In the sister poem, *Byzantium*, Coleridgian
reminders cluster:

> A starlit or a moonlit dome disdains
> All that man is,
> All mere complexities,
> The fury and the mire of human veins.

See how the 'haughty dome'—to quote Byron on St. Peter's—rises
above man's labyrinthine and passionate confusions, as in *Kubla
Khan*. Yeats also glimpses a semi-human shape like the
hermaphrodite-seraphs in Coleridge and Shelley, at once 'shade,'
'image,' and 'man,' referred to the unwinding of maze-paths, itself
beyond *moisture* and *breath*, a 'superhuman' creature of 'death-in-
life' and 'life-in-death.' There are more bird-miracles whose 'glory of
changeless metal' is contrasted with 'complexities of mire and blood.'
'God's holy fire' of our other poem is here expanded into the

Emperor's flames, whereby you can see how God = Emperor = Kubla Khan, Coleridge's monarch:

> At midnight on the Emperor's pavement flit
> Flames that no faggot feeds, nor steel has lit,
> Nor storm disturbs, flames begotten of flame,
> Where blood-begotten spirits come,
> And all complexities of fury leave . . .

They die agonizingly 'into a dance.' The self-generating flames recall the definition of poetry in *Timon of Athens*. When 'spirit after spirit' is seen 'astraddle on the dolphins' mire and blood' we may compare (i) the seraph-forms above dead bodies in *The Ancient Mariner*, and (ii) Shelley's boys riding alligators in *The Witch of Atlas*. The Emperor's 'golden smithies' are said to 'break the flood': that is, annihilate sensual existence. 'Marbles of the dancing floor' now 'break bitter furies of complexity.' The universe is a 'dolphin-torn' and 'gong-tormented' sea. Gong-music suggests eternity-compulsion and relates to the 'great cathedral gong' earlier where its 'resonance' is set between a purified 'night-walker's song' and both 'unpurged images of day' and the Emperor's *drunken* soldiers.

In her fine study *A Servant of the Mightiest* (London, 1927) Mrs. Alfred Wingate describes Kubilai Khan's 'imperial palace' in Peking as a *circular* 'Temple of Heaven' wherein the Emperor as 'Son of Heaven,' mediates between God and man. The description, in no sense derivative from Coleridge's poem, underlines my own interpretations.

A good dome-comment occurs in *The Wisdom of God* by Sergius Bulgakov (London, 1937):

> Anyone who has visited the church of St. Sophia in Constantinople and fallen under the spell of that which it reveals, will find himself permanently enriched by a new apprehension of the world in God, that is, of the Divine Sophia. This heavenly dome, which portrays heaven bending to earth to embrace it, gives expression in finite form to the infinite, to an all-embracing unity, to the stillness of eternity, in the form of a work of art which, though belonging to this world, is a miracle of harmony itself. The grace, lightness, simplicity, and wonderful symmetry of the structure account for the fact that the weight of the dome and even of the very walls seems to dissolve completely. An ocean of light pours in from above and dominates the whole space below—it enchants, convinces, as it seems to say: I am in the world and the world is in me. Here Plato is baptized into

Christianity, for here, surely, we have that lofty realm of his to which souls ascend for the contemplation of ideas.

Later it is called a 'symbol of eternity,' and a 'prophetic symbolism.' Domes are at once prophecy and poetry.

Nevertheless, most of Shakespeare lies outside our present study, his work being peculiarly non-vertical, with comparatively slight emphasis on the sculptural and plastic, though the sonnets provide relevant passages:

Not marble nor the gilded monuments
Of princes shall outlive this powerful rhyme . . .

Tomb-monuments occur occasionally in the plays. Such impressions gain in importance in his final period, corresponding to the concept 'eternity': as in the engraved imagery of *Cymbeline*, Prospero's 'cloud-clapped towers' and 'solemn temples,' and Hermione's *living* statue; and emphasis generally on sacred buildings and religious ritual. Pope, though normally avoiding architectures, concludes his satires with a 'Temple of Eternity' (*Epilogue* 11); and Byron's latest work resembles Shakespeare's in its tendency to plastic, though vital, eternities.

—G. Wilson Knight, *The Starlit Dome: Studies in the Poetry of Vision* (Oxford: Oxford University Press, 1941): pp. 310–13.

⊛

FRANK KERMODE ON BYZANTIUM AS AN IMAGE

[Sir Frank Kermode is a professor of English at Cambridge University. Among his best known books are *Romantic Image; The Classic; The Sense of an Ending; Continuities; Shakespeare, Spenser and Donne: Renaissance Essays; The Uses of Error;* and *The Genesis of Secrecy.* In this extract taken from his book *Romantic Image,* he asserts that Byzantium gave Yeats the sense of an image that transcended human specifications.]

'Sailing to Byzantium' could scarcely be regarded as less than a profoundly considered poem; yet Yeats was willing to accept the criticism of the acute Sturge Moore that the antithesis of the birds of the dying generations and the golden bird was imperfect; and this consideration was one of the causes of the second poem, 'Byzantium.' "Your *Sailing to Byzantium*," wrote Moore, "magnificent as the first three stanzas are, lets me down in the fourth, as such a goldsmith's bird is as much nature as man's body, especially if it only sings like Homer and Shakespeare of what is past or passing or to come to Lords and Ladies." Yeats sent him a copy of 'Byzantium' so that he should have an idea of what was needed for the symbolic cover design of his new book (at this time he was going to call it not *The Winding Stair* but *Byzantium)* and added that Moore's criticism was the origin of the new poem—it had shown the poet that "the idea needed exposition." Only a little earlier, by the way, Moore had provided Yeats with a copy of Flecker's 'A Queen's Song,' which has a certain relevance to 'Byzantium,' being a treatment of the topic of living beauty *versus* bronze and marble, or in this instance, gold:

Had I the power
To Midas given of old
To touch a flower
And leave its petal gold
I then might touch thy face,
Delightful boy,
And leave a metal grace
A graven joy.

Thus would I slay—
Ah! desperate device!—
The vital day
That trembles in thine eyes,
And let the red lips close
Which sang so well
And drive away the rose
To leave a shell.

We have already seen why Yeats was so interested in Byzantine art; it gave him that sense of an image totally estranged from specifically human considerations (and particularly from discursive intellect) with meaning and form identical, the vessel of the spectator's passion, which led him to develop the Dancer image. These lines of Flecker point also towards that life-in-death, death-in-life, which characterises the perfect being of art. The absolute difference, as of different orders of reality, between the Image and what is, in the usual sense, alive, was the crucial point upon which the first

Byzantium poem had, on Moore's view, failed: it was so important to the poet that he did his work again, making the distinction more absolute, seeking some more perfect image to convey the quality, out of nature and life and becoming, of the apotheosized marble and bronze. The bird must absolutely be a bird of artifice; the entire force of the poem for Yeats depended upon this—otherwise he would scarcely have bothered about Moore's characteristic, and of course intelligent, quibble. Professor N. Jeffares has shown how full are the opening lines of 'Sailing to Byzantium' of peculiarly powerful suggestions of natural life, the life of generation; the salmon carries obvious suggestions of sexual vigour, and, it might be added, of that achieved physical beauty Yeats so much admired, immense power and utter singleness of purpose, in the business of generating and dying. Of course the golden bird must be the antithesis of this, as well as the heavenly counterpart of old scarecrows. It prophesies, speaks out as the foolish and passionate need not; it uses the language of courtesy in a world where all the nature-enforced discriminations of spirit and body, life and death, being and becoming, are meaningless. "Marbles of the dancing floor / Break bitter furies of complexity". And it is this world that Byzantium symbolises. Mr. Jeffares says the bird is different in the second poem because "here it is explicitly contrasted with natural birds, to their disadvantage." In fact the same contrast is intended in the earlier poem; the new degree of explicitness is what Moore's criticism forced upon the poet. The focus of attention is no longer on the poignancy of the contrast between nature and art in these special senses; nature now becomes "mere complexities, The fury and the mire," and the strategy of the poem is, clearly, to establish the immense paradoxical vitality of the dead, more alive than the living; still, but richer in movement than the endless agitation of becoming.

And this is precisely the concept of the dead face and the dancer, the mind moving like a top, which I am calling the central icon of Yeats and of the whole tradition. Byzantium is where this is the normal condition, where all is image and there are no contrasts and no costs, inevitable concomitants of the apparition of absolute being in the sphere of becoming. We can harm the poem by too exclusive an attention to its eschatology, and it is salutary to read it simply as a marvellously contrived emblem of what Yeats took the work of art to be. There is no essential contradiction between the readings. The reconciling force is Imagination, the creator of the symbol by which men "dream and so create Translunar paradise." Or, to use the completely appropriate language of Blake, "This world of Imagination is the world of Eternity; it is the divine bosom into which we shall all go after the death of the Vegetated body. This World of Imagination is Infinite & Eternal, whereas the world of Generation, or Vegetation, is Finite & Temporal . . . The Human Imagination . . . appear'd to Me . . . throwing off the Temporal that the Eternal might be Establish'd . . . In Eternity one Thing never Changes into another Thing. Each Identity is Eternal". There is no better gloss on Yeats's poem, a poem impossible outside the tradition of the Romantic Image and its corollary, the doctrine of necessary isolation and suffering in the artist.

—Frank Kermode, *Romantic Image* (London: Routledge & Keegan Paul, 1957): pp. 87–89.

☙

Helen Hennessy Vendler on the Opposing Images in the Poem

[Helen Hennessy Vendler is the A. Kingley Porter University Professor at Harvard University. Her books include *On Extended Wings: Wallace Stevens's Longer Poems* (1969), *Part of Nature, Part of Us* (1981), *The Odes of John Keats* (1983), and *The Given and the Made: Strategies of Poetic Redefinition* (1996). In this extract taken from her book on Yeats, published in 1963, she shows how Yeats uses the ideas of purgation and immortality as symbols for his creative experience.]

Yeats wanted to identify Phase 15 with Byzantium; by this identification Christ becomes the artist who, in choosing "perfection of the work" makes possible the glories of Hagia Sophia. The full moon of Byzantium makes a Christ of stern majesty whose "Byzantine eyes of drilled ivory staring upon a vision" show affinities to the plummet-measured face of the statues. Remote and harsh, ascetic and hieratic, the image of Byzantium is the one transcendent glimpse in *A Vision*, and deservedly the most famous of Yeats's mythical symbols. In *A Vision*, Yeats permits himself the tone of wonder and repose in his descriptions of the sacred city, but in the poems, he is wrenched from his contemplation by the importunities of the body. The tattered coat upon a stick acts as a counterpoise to the sages standing in God's holy fire, and "Byzantium" is a poem tortured by the antitheses it confronts, where "the fury and the mire of human veins" always inundate the marbles of the dancing floor.

Because "Byzantium" is Yeats's most authoritative poetic word on Phase 15, I do not want to bypass the poem without comment. It is, I think, Yeats's greatest single triumph; in it, that sense of agonizing balance between opposites which was his primary poetic intuition receives its most acute rendering. "Byzantium" is a poem about the images in a poet's mind, and this in itself implies that perhaps *A Vision* may be about images too, at least in part. Images are the raw material of poetry, and Yeats divides them into two varieties, purged and unpurged. The unpurged are those belonging to the daytime, to the random mass of heterogeneous experience, and they contain

All that man is,
All mere complexities
The fury and the mire of human veins.

The purged images are those of night. Yeats calls one of them, paraphrasing Dante's address to Virgil. "shade more than man, more image than a shade," and we conclude that these images do not have even the shadowy humanity of the spirits of Hades, but rather are dehumanized "bobbins" without moisture or breath. As superhuman beings, they have affinities with the Jove who visited Leda, or with any other visitants from supernatural regions. Any image, once arisen, can bring others in its train:

A mouth that has no moisture and no breath
Breathless mouths may summon.

Images have this in common with the mask: they are opposites of the poet who invokes them, they are the creations of his desire. Will and mask exist always in the Heraclitean relationship, "living each other's death, dying each other's life," and therefore Yeats addresses his image in a conscious recollection of Coleridge:

I hail the superhuman;
I call it death-in-life and life-in-death.

The purged images of night are associated with the holy city of Byzantium, and when the gong strikes, "the unpurged images of day recede," while the starlit or moonlit dome disdains the complexities it banishes. The dome may be starlit (at Phase 1) or moonlit (at Phase 15); the perfect objective and the perfect subjective are alike independent of "the fury and the mire of human veins." The golden bird (who is probably the golden nightingale of "Sailing to Byzantium") scorns aloud the "common bird or petal / And all complexities of mire or blood." Like the floating superhuman image, the golden nightingale is refined almost beyond recognition; just as the image was "Shade more than man, more image than a shade," so the nightingale is "More miracle than bird or handiwork."

—Helen Hennessy Vendler, *Yeats's* Vision *and the Later Plays* (Cambridge, Mass.: Harvard University Press, 1963): pp. 113–15.

⊗

Thomas R. Whitaker on the Ambiguities in "Byzantium"

[Thomas R. Whitaker is a professor at Yale University and author of a book on William Carlos Williams (1968), as well as *Mirrors or Our Playing: Paradigms and Presences in Modern Drama* (1999). In this extract taken from his study on Yeats, *Swan and Shadow: Yeats's Dialogue with History* (1964), he discusses the ambiguities of the poem.]

Similar paradoxes appear in "Sailing to Byzantium," in which a voyage to a specific point in history is a Plotinian voyage beyond all history, and in which monuments of the soul's magnificence reveal sages standing in God's holy fire. The generic "Soul" comes to seem both egocentric and transcendent, and the carefully unspecified golden "form" for which the speaker yearns suggests both human construct and Platonic idea. As an imagined transmutation of the active and passionate speaker into the realm of transcendental contemplation, that form also invites comparison with the iconography of the Mundaka Upanishad: "Like two birds of golden plumage, inseparable companions, the individual self and the immortal Self are perched on the branches of the selfsame tree. The former tastes of the sweet and bitter fruits of the tree; the latter, tasting of neither, calmly observes." By the end of the poem the speaker has almost reached the point where the two birds—soulbird and sunbird, the yearning old man and the golden form—become one: in the striving yet contemplative voice that sings of "what is past, and passing, and to come" within *this* "artifice of eternity." The poem thus evokes that Phoenix nest upon the Tree of Life (as Yeats described it in another passage dealing with the same cluster of symbols) which holds "the passion that is exaltation and the negation of the will." It fuses what he, like Schopenhauer, called the two halves of the soul.

"Byzantium," of course, elaborates yet more richly these ambiguities of craft and inspiration, creation of new life and death to this life, in that realm inhabited by

> image, man or shade,
> Shade more than man, more image than a shade

as by

> Miracle, bird or golden handiwork,
> More miracle than bird or handiwork . . .

In each poem the speaker moves on his winding path or whirlpool-turning toward the timeless, through the sea of generation toward the condition of fire, which descends to meet him by way of its own gyre or winding path. Then may occur on the pavement of Byzantium what Blake had described as occurring in his "Holy City":

> From the clotted gore & from the hollow den
> Start forth the trembling millions into flames of mental fire,
> Bathing their limbs in the bright visions of Eternity.

That archetypal image of spiralling mutual approach, embodied in a long tradition of ritual and iconography, is an apt symbol for the paradoxes of Yeats's creative perception. The meeting point of the two gyres may suggest that combination of incarnation and transfiguration which occurs when the poem itself translates the turbulent *rota* of history into passionate stillness, the "gong-tormented sea" of "mire and blood" into "an agony of flame," or Blake's "Bloody Deluge" into "living flames winged with intellect."

—Thomas R. Whitaker, *Swan and Shadow: Yeats's Dialogue with History* (Chapel Hill: The University of North Carolina Press, 1964): pp. 111–12.

RICHARD ELLMANN ON THE OPPOSING IMAGES IN THE POEM

[Richard Ellmann was Goldsmiths' Professor of English at New College, Oxford. He is the foremost scholar of Joyce and Yeats. This excerpt is taken from his book *The Identity of Yeats*. Here he discusses Yeats's handling of difficult images.]

'Byzantium' is a dramatic example of Yeats's handling of the image, and a difficult one. At first the poet appears to distinguish between two meanings of the word. In the beginning stanza, 'The unpurged images of day recede.' These day-time images, which the poet so immediately dismisses, are apparently the ordinary objects of experience which make up the external world. Only at the end of the poem do we learn that they are made of the same stuff as the night-time images, one of which he now proceeds to invoke:

Before me floats an image, man or shade,
Shade more than man, more image than a shade.

Such images seem at first to be far removed from life, since they are identifiable neither with the living man nor his ghostly substitute.

How may the poet grasp these images, as he must do if his poetry is to go below the superficies of day? Yeats answers with two powerful affirmations:

For Hades' bobbin bound in mummy-cloth
May unwind the winding path;
A mouth that has no moisture and no breath
Breathless mouths may summon. . . .

Hades' bobbin is the soul, which comes from the underworld and eventually returns there until its rebirth. In life it winds up the mummy-cloth of experience, a funereal term used because in the poem life is paradoxically regarded as a surrender of the soul's freedom and therefore as a kind of imprisonment or death. On returning to Hades the soul unwinds the cloth—'the winding path' of nature—like a bobbin unwinding thread. But, says the poet, even during life, at moments of 'breathless' inspiration, we escape from ourselves and our past and summon the deathless, lifeless image which 'has no moisture and no breath.'

I hail the superhuman;
I call it death-in-life and life-in-death.

From the point of view of this life, such images are dead; but from a more detached vantage-point, it is they that are immortal, and the living who have no genuine life.

In the next stanza the poet's eye fastens on another superhuman image; by ecstatically defining it as 'miracle, bird, or golden handiwork,' he locates it more precisely in the world of art. He thinks of it as having a bird's shape, and as either crowing like the cocks of Hades or scorning other birds and life. Yeats had learned from Eugénie Strong's *Apotheosis and After Life* that the cock, as herald of the sun, became 'by an easy transition the herald of rebirth' on Roman tombstones. Since in this poem he accepts reincarnation, he is distinguishing here between the birds that sing the common strain of the continuing cycle of human lives and those that scorn the cycle and sing only of escape from it; here were the two directions of his own art.

There follows a sudden revelation of the process by which such images are hammered out, by the Byzantine smithies of the imagination, into their purest form:

At midnight on the Emperor's pavement flit
Flames that no faggot feeds, nor steel has lit,
Nor storm disturbs, flames begotten of flame,
Where blood-begotten spirits come
And all complexities of fury leave,
Dying into a dance,
An agony of trance,
An agony of flame that cannot singe a sleeve.

Begotten by the living, they have to be immortalized by fire. Some aspects of their perfected state are clarified in notes which Yeats made for *A Vision* two years before writing 'Byzantium':

At first we are subject to Destiny . . . but the point in the Zodiac where the whirl becomes a sphere once reached, we may escape from the constraint of our nature and from that of external things, entering upon a state where all fuel has become flame, where there is nothing but the state itself, nothing to constrain it or end it. We attain it always in the creation or enjoyment of a work of art, but that moment though eternal in the Daimon passes from us because it is not an attainment of our whole being. Philosophy has always explained its moment of moments in much the same way; nothing can be added to it, nothing taken away; that all progressions are full of illusion, that everything is born there like a ship in full sail.

By equating the perfection of the afterlife with every metaphysical perfection the philosophers have conceived and with the perfection of art wrought 'in nature's spite,' Yeats avoids mere estheticism and justifies the description in 'Byzantium' which treats the passage of the spirits of the dead to the other world and their purification there as synonymous with the purgative process which a work of art undergoes. These processes are among those which Yeats makes equivalent and symbolical of one another.

But the fires of the imagination have a characteristic which distinguishes them from the fires of this world: they burn and do not burn. They are all-powerful to purge images of any experiential dross, but impotent to singe a sleeve. In a position of prominence in the poem, the last line of the above stanza, Yeats casts one of the many backward glances in his poetry, directing it here towards the life of action that the spirit or image is transcending. At the very moment that he heralds the purgative process, he reminds us that the purgation can occur only outside action, for there it has no power. The same reflection causes him, at the end of the poem, to express not his admiration for the completed work, as might be expected, but his wonder at the spawning images, covered with the mire of experience, in which the work began:

> Marbles of the dancing-floor
> Break bitter furies of complexity,
> Those images that yet
> Fresh images beget,
> That dolphin-torn, that gong-tormented sea.

Ecstatic before the perfection of the creative process, the poet still yields a little to the fascination for the imperfect and unpurged images not yet arrived at Byzantium.

For Yeats is more the poet of the sea torn by sexuality and tormented by time than the poet of the perfect moment. He frequently represents himself as on the verge of renouncing those poetic vows which have kept him from the life of action, as in a letter to Ethel Mannin of November 15, 1936, 'All my life it has been hard to keep from action, as I wrote when a boy, "To be not of the things I dream."' To write his poems he had reluctantly 'brayed my life in a mortar,' he reported, when he was less than twenty-four, to Katharine Tynan. His anxiety over this dilemma lent poignancy to the otherwise glib antithesis, 'The intellect of man is forced to choose / Perfection of the life or of the work.' The same undercurrent, of a reaction from perfection, that appears in 'Byzantium,' appears in many other poems, notably 'Vacillation,' 'The Grey Rock,' and 'Meditations in Time of Civil War.'

—Richard Ellmann, *The Identity of Yeats* (New York: Oxford University Press, 1964): pp. 219–23.

Thematic Analysis of
"Cuchulain Comforted"

Yeats wrote this poem two weeks before his death. Dated January 13, 1939, it first appeared in the volume *Last Poems and Two Plays*, which was posthumously published the same year.

The prose draft of the poem gives a detailed account of what was to become the poem. (The full version is given in A. N. Jeffares's commentary among the Critical Extracts.) In his letter to Edith Shackleton Heald, Yeats wrote that he was making "a prose sketch—a kind of sequel—strange, too, something new." As the prose sketch suggests, Yeats had Dante's *Inferno* in mind while he was writing the poem. Yeats even composed the poem in a Dante-style *terza rima*, a verse form with which he had little experience, another indication that Yeats was trying to match his "much-loved master," Dante.

In this difficult and impressive death poem, Yeats turns to Cuchulain, the most distinguished warrior of the Ulster Cycle of Irish stories. The image of Cuchulain haunted Yeats for years; in fact, the hero appeared in five of Yeats's plays. In the poem, Yeats bestows on Cuchulain an image of heroic completeness with the strange overtones of lines 16–20 from Canto XV of Dante's *Inferno*, which read:

> A company of shades came into sight
> walking beside the bank. They stared at us ⟨...⟩
>
> ⟨...⟩ pointing their eyebrows toward us
> as an old tailor squints at his needle's eye.

The poem's opening is:

> A man that had six wounds, a man
> Violent and famous, strode among the dead;
> Eyes stared out of the branches and were gone.

Cuchulain, who had faced challenge after challenge in real life, is now striding among the dead. He is next shown leaning against a tree, disinclined to submit himself to the world in a valley of the dead. He reflects on love and war: "He leant upon a tree / As though to meditate on wounds and blood."

Then spirits, "certain Shrouds," described as "bird-like things," bring a bundle of linen before him. They are the opposites of the great hero:

> 'But first you must be told our character:
> Convicted cowards all by kindred slain
> Or driven from home and left to die in fear.'

And they are frightened of him:

> Mainly because of what we know
> The rattle of those arms makes us afraid.

Whatever they do, we are told, they always act collectively. They are occupied in sewing shrouds, and they ask Cuchulain to make a garment resembling the ones they are wearing: "'We thread the needles' eyes, and all we do / All must together do.'" When Cuchulain takes the nearest needle and begins to sew, the shades announce, "'Now must we sing and sing the best we can.'" Yeats then writes, "They sang but had not human tunes nor words, / Though all was done in common as before." After this comes Yeats's magnificent line, "They had changed their throats and had the throats of birds." This is similar to a stage direction at the end of Yeats's play *The Death of Cuchulain:* "There is a silence, and in the silence, a few faint bird notes."

Many baffling questions arise from the poem: Why is Cuchulain, who lived and died heroically, among cowards? How can he be "comforted" if he is among them? Is the title ironic? Is the poem comforting? What is the tonality of the poem?

The poem also raises other, more specific questions about its imagery: What is the meaning of the shroud? Does it represent the celestial body? What does the needle's eye, an image that Yeats uses in some of his other poems, stand for? Does it derive from the New Testament? Perhaps it represents the gateway to Paradise, relating to Jesus' statement in Matthew 19: "It is easier for a camel to go through the eye of a needle than for a rich man to enter the kingdom of God." Issues such as these have puzzled the critics and generated a great deal of debate. Most of the questions remain without definitive answers.

What matters is that poetry, at its greatest, deals with subjects on the edge of thought and emotion, meaning that we cannot know it until we are willing to listen to the mysterious tide beneath its surface. That is why Yeats's poetry is best read aloud and even memorized if possible. Only then can we become aware of the infinite complexity of Yeats's orchestrations of sound and delicate meaning. ❀

Critical Views on
"Cuchulain Comforted"

F. A. C. Wilson on Yeats's Theory of the Daemon

[F. A. C. Wilson is the author of *Yeats's Iconography* (1960) and *Six Essays on the Development of T. S. Eliot* (1960). This extract is taken from his book *W. B. Yeats and Tradition*. Here he discusses how the full understanding of this poem depends on knowledge of Yeats's theory of "daemons" as guardian angels.]

'Cuchulain Comforted' depends for its full understanding on Yeats's theory of the daemon, which is perhaps his most significant departure from orthodox Platonic theory, and as such is best set out in some detail before we approach the text. Yeats's interest in the theory of the daemon (or guardian angel; though there are perverse daemons as well as good) originated, beyond theosophy, from Blake, who thought that all human achievement emanated from man's 'genius' 'which by the ancients was called an Angel and Spirit and Demon.' Yeats's cardinal authority was Plutarch, who taught him that 'good spirits change always for the best,' and are transformed in course of time into angels or daemons, 'and from Daemons, by degrees and in a long course of time, a few souls being refined and purified come to partake of the nature of the Divinity.' Plutarch thought that it was the province of the daemon to care for and encourage humanity:

> Those souls, as Hesiod says, that are not to be put into another body, but are forced from all union with flesh, turn guardian Daemons, and preside over others; for as wrestlers, when old age makes them unfit for exercise, have some love for it still left, delight to see others wrestle, and encourage them; so souls that have passed all the stages of life, and by their virtue are exalted into Daemons, do not slight the endeavours of man, but being kind to those that strive for the same attainments, and in some sort banding and siding with them, encourage and help them on, when they see them near their hope and ready to catch the desired prize.

He taught that the daemon communicated with men 'in sleep,' and sometimes in a waking trance condition, not as 'an apparition, but rather a sensible perception of a voice; as in a dream there is no real voice, yet we have fancies and apprehensions of words which make us imagine that we hear someone speak.' Plutarch's theory was (I think) an influence upon medieval Christian angelology, which is well known in some respects to connect with Platonic teachings; and similar views on divine communication came to be expressed by Donne, who in 'Air and Angels' tells us how 'angels' often manifest 'in a voice.' Accepting all this as he did, Yeats had therefore ample precedent.

Where Yeats differed from Plutarch (and 'Cuchulain Comforted' cannot be understood apart from this) was in respect of the relation between man and his daemon. For Plutarch and Platonism generally, the daemon came to a man as like to like, 'to those that strive for the same attainments.' But Yeats applied to Plutarch's thesis the theory of opposites of Heraclitus, and suggested that the daemon was never man's similar, always his opposite.

> Plutarch's precepts . . . have it that a strange living man may win for Daemon an illustrious dead man; but now I add another thought: the Daemon comes not as like to like but seeking its own opposite, for man and Daemon feed the hunger in one another's hearts.

As I have said, Yeats thought of the spiritual and the human as both opposite and complementary, each needing the other to attain to completeness; and he imagined that the daemon was irresistibly attracted to whatever man was possessed of the qualities which, in life, it had itself lacked. Thus, man and daemon each completed the other's experience, and the daemon, from its own past knowledge, was able to lead the man on to his destiny: 'among things not impossible, whatever is most difficult.' Whatever seemed difficult to the man would be well within the guardian angel's reach. ⟨. . .⟩

We are now in a position to look at the poem in full detail. Cuchulain is shown leaning against a tree in a valley of the dead, violent and turbulent in purgatory as in life, unwilling to reconcile himself to the new world around him, and continuing, in death, to 'meditate on wounds and blood.' Certain spirits come out from the trees to meet him; they are described as 'bird-like things,' and are reminiscent, perhaps, of the bird-headed ghosts of Egyptian theurgy, where, before the *psychostasia*, souls also pass through a valley of the dead. These spirits describe themselves in terms which make it clear that they are the 'great fighting man's' opposites:

'... first you must be told our character:
Convicted cowards all, by kindred slain
Or driven from home and left to die in fear.'

If we now apply the knowledge of Yeats's theory of the soul which we possess, it will be very clear that these spirits are Cuchulain's guardian angels or daemons, to whom he is in process of being united after death. Even so, and as we shall see, he still has need of their help.

—F. A. C. Wilson, *W. B. Yeats and Tradition* (New York: The Macmillan Company, 1958): pp. 244–45, 247–48.

A. Norman Jeffares on a Draft of the Poem

[A. Norman Jeffares has written extensively on Yeats and is one of the most well-known and respected Yeatsian scholars. In this extract, taken from his *A Commentary on the Collected Poems of W. B. Yeats,* he gives his interpretation of some lines of the poem.]

The poem is related to Yeats's play *The Death of Cuchulain.* It may be the poem for which Yeats wrote to Edith Shackleton Heald on 1 January 1939 that he was making 'a prose sketch for a poem—a kind of sequel—strange too, something new.' It is possible that it may also be the lyric arising out of the play mentioned in an earlier letter to her of December 1938. The prose draft, according to Mrs. Yeats, was dictated on 7 January 1939.

Dorothy Wellesley gives an account of the prose version of the poem:

> On one of our visits to him at Cap Martin he read the prose theme of a poem he proposed to write in *terza rima:*
> A shade recently arrived went through a valley in the Country of the Dead; he had six mortal wounds, but had been a tall, strong, handsome man. Other shades looked at him from among the trees. Sometimes they went near to him and then went away quickly. At last he sat down, he seemed very tired. Gradually the shades gathered round him, and one of them who seemed to have some authority among the others laid a parcel of linen at his feet. One of the others

said: 'I am not so afraid of him now that he is sitting still. It was the way his arms rattled.' Then another shade said: 'You would be much more comfortable if you would make a shroud and wear it instead of the arms. We have brought you some linen. If you make it yourself you will be much happier, but of course we will thread the needles. We do everything together, so everyone of us will thread the needles, so when we have laid them at your feet you will take whichever you like best.' The man with six wounds saw that nobody had ever threaded needles so swiftly and so smoothly. He took the threaded needles and began to sew, and one of the shades said: 'We will sing to you while you sew; but you will like to know who we are. We are the people who run away from the battles. Some of us have been put to death as cowards, but others have hidden, and some even died without people knowing they were cowards.' Then they began to sing, and they did not sing like men and women, but like linnets that had been stood on a perch and taught by a good singing master.

⟨Line⟩ 20 *our character*: the account of disincarnate state in ⟨*A Vision*⟩ may be germane to this poem. Yeats is there pondering upon the famous elemental of Leap Castle, and the transformation of the cowards into birds may echo his suggestions in that portion of *AV* about the spirit's relationship with the Celestial or the Passionate Body.

—A. Norman Jeffares, *A Commentary on the Collected Poems of W. B. Yeats* (Stanford: Stanford University Press, 1968): pp. 512–14.

⊛

HELEN HENNESSY VENDLER ON THE ANTITHESIS IN THE POEM

[Helen Hennessy Vendler is the A. Kingley Porter University Professor at Harvard University. Her books include *On Extended Wings: Wallace Stevens's Longer Poems* (1969), *Part of Nature, Part of Us* (1981), *The Odes of John Keats* (1983), and *The Given and the Made: Strategies of Poetic Redefinition* (1996). In this extract taken from her book on Yeats, published in 1963, she says that the poem offers intellectual consolation.]

We may now return to the poem itself, which is an unsettling one in all respects. It is called "Cuchulain Comforted" and we might think of things which had comforted Cuchulain in the past: the joy of battle, the love of women, pride in his son, independence, and sovereignty. What comforts him in the poem is none of these, but rather the communal and timid sewing of a shroud. The antithesis is clear enough, but by it we are made to realize that this purgatory is very different from the otherworld in which Cuchulain moved during his bewitchment by Fand. That bewitchment corresponded to the *Meditation* (containing the Dreaming Back, the Return, and the Phantasmagoria) described in *A Vision*; this purgatory rather corresponds to the *Shiftings*. I give again the passage I quoted in Chapter III:

> At the end of the *Return* . . . the *Spirit* is freed from pleasure and pain and is ready to enter the *Shiftings* where it is freed from Good and Evil, and in this state which is a state of intellect, it lives through a life which is said to be in all things opposite to that lived through in the world, and dreamed through in the *Return* . . . This is brought about by no external law but by a craving in the *Principles* to know what life has hidden, that the *Daimon* who knows intellect but not good and evil, may be satisfied . . . All now is intellect and he [the man] is all *Daimon*, and tragic and happy circumstance alike offer an intellectual ecstasy at the revelation of truth, and the most horrible tragedy in the end can but seem a figure in a dance.

Yeats adds, we recall, that in the *Shiftings* the soul is brought "to quiescence," and this is what comforts Cuchulain. ⟨. . .⟩

It is necessary to realize that the Shrouds are not in the same purgatorial state as Cuchulain. He is learning what cowardice is like by being placed among cowards, and is therefore undergoing the *Shiftings*, while they are probably still in some stage of the *Meditation*, not yet having cast off entirely what they were in life. I do not think that they are "pure souls who have escaped from the round of birth and death," as Wilson would have it; they are far too timid, mindful of their former life, and submerged in common activity to be freed spirits. Nor do they yet sing with the effortlessness of the golden nightingale, but must "sing the best [they] can." Yet they have a lesson to teach Cuchulain, paralleling the lesson that the dice-throwers teach in their dance at the end of *Calvary*—that one must watch one form of life succeed another with detachment, like the three old men in "Lapis Lazuli." That is the only comfort to be found for tragedy, and Yeats insists on it:

All things fall and are built again,
And those that build them again are gay.

The thought was in Yeats's mind at the time he wrote "Cuchulain Comforted" and it completes his tragedy of Cuchulain if we are to believe his words in *On the Boiler*: "The arts are all the bridal chambers of joy. No tragedy is legitimate unless it leads some great character to his final joy."

Cuchulain himself was hardly led to his final joy in *The Death of Cuchulain*, except in his momentary vision of his soul. The poem incarnates that vision, but in an odd way, and I think we are right to be discomfited by such an end for Cuchulain. It leaves him suspended in the otherworld among his opposites, participating in a life which reminds us uncomfortably of the Christian life in *Calvary*: timid, resigned, communal, obedient. There is no suggestion of the resurgence of the hero after such discipline; the poem is almost an abdication of the heroic life in favor of the mild and persuasive placidity of the Shrouds. I do not agree with Mrs. Bjersby that Yeats "is Cuchulain linen-shrouded, and his comfort is that in spite of all—even though he might be counted among the crowd of cowards—he may look upon himself as a hero of the spiritual intellect." There is no hint of such heroism in the poem.

We must realize that the death of Cuchulain symbolized for Yeats roughly what the death of Christ symbolized for Christians. Cuchulain is the antithetical man, and his death is the end of an antithetical age. Another age, whose tutelary spirits will be not unlike the Shrouds, will follow, and with that primary age Yeats is profoundly out of sympathy, for all his attempts at detachment. "Cuchulain Comforted" is a poem of intellectual consolation at change, telling us that a dead end has been reached, and any further development of the image of Cuchulain along previous lines will be fruitless. He must be buried for the time being, change his shape, undergo a purgatorial transformation, and then be resurrected. We are meant to find it a good sign that when we last see Cuchulain he is in Purgatory, since it guarantees his rebirth.

—Helen Hennessy Vendler, Yeats's Vision *and the Later Plays* (Cambridge, Mass.: Harvard University Press, 1963): pp. 249, 250–52.

[This extract is taken from Harold Bloom's Introduction to the volume on Yeats (1986) in Chelsea House's MODERN CRITICAL VIEWS series. Here he compares Gnostic and Yeatsian eschatology.]

I would choose, as Yeats's finest achievement in the Sublime, his death-poem, "Cuchulain Comforted," a Dantesque vision of judgment that is Yeats's condensed equivalent of *The Fall of Hyperion* and *The Triumph of Life*. The prose draft of this poem identifies the shades as being of three kinds, all cowards: "Some of us have been put to death as cowards, but others have hidden, and some even died without people knowing they were cowards. . . ." When Yeats versified the poem, he omitted this last group, thus giving us a hint as to a repressed element in this last daemonic Sublime of his life.

The poem's beautiful last line is its *apophrades*, echoing Dante's Brunetto Latini, who is described as being among the victorious, though justly placed among the damned in the Inferno. As I have shown in my book on Yeats, the poem places itself rather precisely, in terms of *A Vision*'s systematic mapping-out of the phases of the life-after-death. The shades have passed through what Yeats calls the *Meditation,* and have purged themselves of everything in their past incarnations except their sense of cowardice. They are at the very end of the state Yeats names as the *Shiftings,* until in the poem's last line they pass out of the *Shiftings* and enter into the state of *Beatitude.* Cuchulain, type of the hero, "a man / Violent and famous," is a stage behind them, and so needs to be instructed by them, in an heroic irony on Yeats's part that is much more a figure-of-thought than a figure-of-speech. Cuchulain, at the poem's start, is passing out of the *Phantasmagoria,* the third and last stage of the *Meditation,* and has entered the *Shiftings* as soon as he accepts instruction, takes up a needle, and begins to sew the shroud that marks his acceptance of passing-over into his antithesis, the world in which heroism and cowardice blend together as one communal ecstasy.

I think it palpable that "Cuchulain Comforted" is a much better poem than "The Second Coming" and "Byzantium," for it seems wholly coherent and they do not, but I think also that its majestic, chastened Sublimity is necessarily the consequence of a completer repression than the earlier poems indicate, and moreover a repression in which there is less disavowal or negation. The mystery of "Cuchulain Comforted" is concealed in the implications of its view of the afterlife, where what appears to matter is not at all how you behaved in your last incarnation, but what you *know*, as the leader of the shades says, implying strongly that this knowledge is only attained in the afterlife. Certainly this is Gnosis again, though of a peculiarly original sort, firmly based upon Yeats's own mythology of death as worked out in Book III, "The Soul in Judgment," of *A Vision*.

Gnostic eschatology, particularly of the Valentinian sect, is close to Yeatsian eschatology in its larger outlines, though certainly not in any detail. A good motto to "Cuchulain Comforted" would be the best-known Valentinian formula of salvation, significant for its differences as well as its similarities to the poem:

> What liberates is the knowledge of who we were, what we became; where we were, whereunto we have been thrown; whereto we speed, wherefrom we are redeemed; what birth is, and what rebirth.

"Equipped with this *gnosis*," Hans Jonas observes, "the soul after death travels upwards, leaving behind at each sphere the psychical 'vestment' contributed by it." As in Yeats's System, this journey of the *pneuma* has no relation whatsoever to moral conduct in the fallen world, for Yeats and the Gnostics share the same antinomianism. Since Yeats's theoretical human values were always of a kind that made him abstractly welcome Fascist violence, whenever it became available for his approval, we need not to be surprised that his self-punishment, in his purgatorial death-poem, involves a leveling equation of what he believed to be the highest virtue, heroism, with its antithesis in shameful cowardice. We encounter here a repetition of the closing vision of Browning's "Childe Roland," where Roland, like Cuchulain the hero, is blent with his opposites, the band of brothers who were cowards or traitors, into one Condition of Fire. There is both a repression and a self-recognition that Browning and Yeats share. ⟨. . .⟩

How do Browning and Yeats compare upon our scale of poetic repression, that is, in the catachreses and grotesqueries and hyperbolical visions that we have judged to characterize an even more repressed Sublime? Though Browning is reputed to be primarily a poet of the Grotesque, and Yeats has little such reputation, they will be found to be very nearly equal in the figurations of an acute primal repressiveness. Both turned to dramatizations of the self, Browning in monologues and Yeats in lyrics and lyrical plays, in order to evade the prime precursor's romances of the self, but the death-drive of poems like "Alastor" and *Adonais* was detoured by them only in part. Browning repressed his memories of the kind of cowardice he had shown in his early confrontation with his mother and, through her, with the supernaturalist strictures of Evangelicalism. But the figurations produced by this poetic repression were the catachreses of self-ruining, of all those failed questers of whom Roland is the most Sublime. Yeats's repressed cowardice is more mysterious, biographically speaking, and we will need unauthorized biographies before we know enough about it to understand how it came to undergo the magnificent distortions and haunting estrangements of his greatest poems. We can see, now, that his Gnostic tendencies aided Yeats by giving him a wider context in a traditional ontology, however heterodox, for his own *antithetical* longings, since the Yeatsian *antithetical*, like the Nietzschean, can be defined as the ultimate resistance against the almost irresistible force of a primal repression, or as a fixation upon precursors whose integrity was finally a little too terrifying. Shelley and Schopenhauer were questers, in their very different ways, who could journey through the Void without yielding to the temptation of worshiping the Void as itself being sacred. Yeats, like Nietzsche, implicitly decided that he too would rather have the Void as purpose, than be void of purpose.

—Harold Bloom, Introduction to *William Butler Yeats* (New York: Chelsea House Publishers, 1986): pp. 18–20, 22.

Works by
William Butler Yeats

Mosada: A Dramatic Poem. 1886.

The Wanderings of Oisin and Other Poems. 1889.

John Sherman and Dhoya (novel and story). 1891.

The Countess Cathleen and Various Legends and Lyrics. 1892.

The Celtic Twilight (stories). 1893.

The Land of Heart's Desire (verse drama). 1894.

Poems. 1895.

The Secret Rose (stories). 1897.

The Wind among the Reeds. 1899.

The Shadowy Waters (verse drama). 1900.

Cathleen ni Houlihan (verse drama). 1902.

Where There Is Nothing (play). 1902.

Ideas of Good and Evil (essays). 1903.

In the Seven Woods. 1903.

The Hour-Glass: A Morality (play). 1903.

The Hour-Glass and Other Plays. 1904.

The King's Threshold and On Baile's Strand (verse dramas). 1904.

Stories of Red Hanrahan (stories). 1905.

Poems 1899–1905. 1906.

The Poetical Works. 2 vol. 1906–07.

Deirdre (verse drama). 1907.

Discoveries: A Volume of Essays. 1907.

The Unicorn from the Stars and Other Plays (with Lady Gregory). 1908.

The Golden Helmet (story). 1908.

The Collected Works in Verse and Prose. 8 vol. 1908.

The Green Helmet and Other Poems. 1910.

Synge and the Ireland of His Time (essay). 1911.

The Cutting of an Agate (essay). 1912.

Poems Written in Discouragement 1912–1913. 1913.

Responsibilities: Poems and a Play. 1914.

Reveries over Childhood and Youth (autobiography). 1915.

Responsibilities and Other Poems. 1916.

The Wild Swans at Coole. 1917.

Per Amica Silentia Lunae (essays). 1918.

Two Plays for Dancers. 1919.

Michael Robartes and the Dancer. 1921.

Four Plays for Dancers. 1921.

The Trembling of the Veil (autobiography). 1922.

Later Poems. 1922.

Plays in Prose and Verse, Written for an Irish Theatre (with Lady
  Gregory). 1922.

The Player Queen (play). 1922.

Plays and Controversies (essays and plays). 1923.

Essays. 1924.

The Cat and the Moon (poems and play). 1924.

The Bounty of Sweden (Nobel lecture). 1924.

Early Poems and Stories. 1925.

A Vision (prose). 1925. (rev. 1937)

October Blast. 1927.

The Tower. 1928.

Sophocles' King Oedipus: A Version for the Modern Stage. 1928.

The Death of Synge and Other Passages from an Old Diary. 1928.

A Packet for Ezra Pound (essay). 1929.

The Winding Stair. 1929.

Words for Music Perhaps and Other Poems. 1932.

The Winding Stair and Other Poems. 1933.

The Collected Poems. 1933.

Letters to the New Island (essays). 1934.

The Words Upon the Window-Pane (play). 1934.

Wheels and Butterflies (plays). 1934.

The Collected Plays. 1934.

The King of the Great Clock Tower (verse drama). 1934.

A Full Moon in March (plays and poems). 1935.

Dramatis Personae (autobiography). 1935.

Poems. 1935.

Nine One-Act Plays. 1937.

Essays, 1931 to 1936. 1937.

The Herne's Egg: A Stage Play. 1938.

New Poems. 1938.

Last Poems and Two Plays. 1939.

On the Boiler (essays). 1939.

Last Poems and Plays. 1940.

If I Were Four-and-Twenty (essay). 1940.

Poems: Definitive Edition. 2 vol. 1949.

The Collected Plays. 1952.

The Variorum Edition of the Poems. Ed. Peter Allt and Russell K. Alspach. 1957.

Mythologies (stories and assorted prose). 1959.

Essays and Introductions. 1961.

Explorations (essays). 1962.

The Variorum Edition of the Plays. Ed. Russell K. Alspach. 1966.

Uncollected Prose. 2 vol. Ed. John P. Frayne. 1970.

Memoirs: Autobiography. Ed. Denis Donoghue. 1972.

The Collected Poems. Revised 2nd ed. Ed. Richard Finneran. 1989.

The Collected Works. 14 vol. (ongoing.) Richard Finneran and George Mills Harper, general eds. 1989–.

Under the Moon: The Unpublished Early Poetry. Ed. George Bornstein. 1995.

Works about
William Butler Yeats

Bloom, Harold. *Yeats.* New York: Oxford University Press, 1970.

———, ed. *William Butler Yeats.* New York: Chelsea House Publishers, 1986.

Bornstein, George. *Yeats and Shelley.* Chicago: The University of Chicago Press, 1970.

———. *Poetic Remaking: The Art of Browning, Yeats, and Pound.* University Park, Pa.: Pennsylvania State University Press, 1988.

Bowra, Maurice. *The Heritage of Symbolism.* London: Macmillan, 1943.

Brooks, Cleanth. "Yeats: The Poet as Myth-Maker." In *Modern Poetry and the Tradition.* Chapel Hill: University of North Carolina Press, 1939.

———. "Yeats's Great Rooted Blossomer." In *The Well-Wrought Urn: Studies in the Structure of Poetry.* New York: Harcourt, Brace and World, 1947.

Davie, Donald. "Yeats, Berkeley, and Romanticism." In *English Literature and British Philosophy,* ed. S. P. Rosenbaum. Chicago: The University of Chicago Press, 1971.

De Man, Paul. "Imagery in Yeats." In *Rhetoric of Romanticism.* New York: Columbia University Press, 1984.

Donoghue, Denis. *William Butler Yeats.* New York: Viking, 1971.

Donoghue, Denis, and J. R. Muryne, eds. *An Honoured Guest: New Essays on W. B. Yeats.* New York: St. Martin's Press, 1966.

Ellmann, Richard. *The Identity of Yeats.* New York: Oxford University Press, 1964.

———. *Yeats: The Man and the Masks.* New York: Macmillan, 1948.

Engelberg, Edward. *The Vast Design: Patterns in W. B. Yeats's Aesthetic.* Toronto: University of Toronto Press, 1964.

Frye, Northrop. "Yeats and the Language of Symbolism." In *Fables of Identity: Studies in Poetic Mythology.* New York: Harcourt, Brace and World, 1963.

————. "The Top of the Tower: A Study of the Imagery of Yeats." In *The Stubborn Structure: Essays on Criticism and Society*. Ithaca, N.Y.: Cornell University Press, 1970.

Gordon, D. J. *W. B. Yeats: Images of a Poet*. Manchester: Manchester University Press, 1962.

Henn, T. R. *The Lonely Tower: Studies in the Poetry of W. B. Yeats*. London: Methuen, 1965.

Jeffares, A. Norman. *W. B. Yeats: Man and Poet*. New York: Barnes and Noble, 1962.

————. *In Excited Reverie: A Century Tribute to William Butler Yeats 1865–1939*. London: Macmillan, 1965.

————. *A Commentary on the Collected Poems of W. B. Yeats*. Stanford, Calif.: Stanford University Press, 1968.

————, ed. *Yeats, Sligo, and Ireland*. Gerrards Cross, Buckinghamshire, U.K.: Colin Smythe, Ltd., 1980.

Kermode, Frank. *Romantic Image*. London: Routledge and Kegan Paul, 1961.

Knight, G. Wilson. *The Starlit Dome: Studies in Poetry of Vision*. Oxford: Oxford University Press, 1941.

Langbaum, Robert. *The Mysteries of Identity: A Theme in Modern Literature*. New York: Oxford University Press, 1977.

Melchiori, Giorgio. *The Whole Mystery of Art: Pattern into Poetry in the Work of W. B. Yeats*. London: Routledge & Kegan Paul, 1960.

Miller, J. Hillis. *Poets of Reality: Six Twentieth-Century Writers*. Cambridge, Mass.: Belknap/Harvard University Press, 1965.

Regueiro, Helen. *The Limits of Imagination: Wordsworth, Yeats, and Stevens*. Ithaca, N.Y.: Cornell University Press, 1976.

Ronsley, Joseph. *Yeats's Autobiography: Life as Symbolic Pattern*. Cambridge, Mass.: Harvard University Press, 1968.

Rudd, Margaret. *Divided Image: A Study of William Blake and W. B. Yeats*. London: Routledge and Kegan Paul, 1953.

Shaw, Priscilla. *Rilke, Valéry, and Yeats: The Domain of the Self*. Rutgers, N.J.: Rutgers University Press, 1964.

Stauffer, A. Donald. *The Golden Nightingale: Essays on Some Principles of Poetry in the Lyrics of W. B. Yeats*. New York: Macmillan, 1949.

Stallworthy, Jon. *Between the Lines: Yeats's Poetry in the Making*. Oxford: Clarendon Press, 1963.

Vendler, Helen Hennessy. *Yeats's* Vision *and the Later Plays*. Cambridge, Mass.: Harvard University Press, 1963.

Wade, A. *A Bibliography of the Writings of W. B. Yeats*. London: Hart-Davis, 1957.

Whitaker, Thomas R. *Swan and Shadow: Yeats's Dialogue with History*. Chapel Hill: University of North Carolina Press, 1964.

Wilson, Edmund. *Axel's Castle*. London: Scribner, 1931.

Zwerdling, Alex. *Yeats and the Heroic Ideal*. New York: New York University Press, 1965.

Index of
Themes and Ideas